THE PRAYER PRINCIPLE

THE PRAYER PRINCIPLE

by

MICHAEL BAUGHEN

Rector of All Souls, Langham Place

MOWBRAY

LONDON & OXFORD

Copyright © Michael Baughen 1981

ISBN 0 264 66701 8

First published 1981
by A. R. Mowbray & Co. Ltd.
Saint Thomas House
Becket Street, Oxford, OX1 1SJ

Computer assisted phototypesetting by
Elanders Limited, Corby, Northants NN17 1PB

Printed in Great Britain by
Richard Clay (The Chaucer Press) Ltd, Bungay, Suffolk

To Myrtle,
And to Rachel, Philip and Andrew
With thanksgiving, love and prayer.

CONTENTS

INTRODUCTION

In the first four months of 1978 we preached a series of sermons at All Souls, Langham Place entitled 'Business with God in Prayer.' It had considerable effect on the preachers and the hearers. We have a Team Ministry and the series was shared with me by Graham Claydon and Andrew Cornes, with one sermon by John Stott. We learnt from one another and I readily acknowledge the benefit I received from my colleagues' ministry, which is bound to be reflected in the contents of this book. After the series I 'went back to square one' and thought through the whole subject again at some length for conference ministry. The conference addresses that resulted have led to this book. I am grateful to all who have helped me down the years, not least in the matter of prayer. I am grateful to my present colleagues at All Souls – John Stott, Graham Claydon, Andrew Cornes, Richard Inwood and Roger Simpson – and for all they teach me in the work of the ministry. I am grateful too for the stimulus, vitality, support and fellowship of the members of the church family at All Souls – a church family that has prayer as the central hub of its life – and I thank them for all they teach me about prayer.

My warm thanks also to David Winter for his editorial encouragement, to Pippa Dobson, Susan Rybarchyk and Vivienne Curry for typing the manuscript, to Mowbray* for publishing it and especially to my wife, Myrtle, for all her help and encouragement.

Michael Baughen

*(and to Harold Shaw Publishers in the USA)

SECTION ONE

START WITH GOD

1 GO BACK TO *START*

'Let's start at the very beginning – it's a very good place to start!' That wise advice for learning the sound of music is also true for learning how to pray. You know how it is when you come home and enter the family lounge. The rest of the family are engrossed in the television play but you have come in half way through. 'Who's he?' you ask. 'Why is the man running? What's the reason for that?' The rest of the family hush you up. They know what is going on and they don't want to miss anything by having to explain to you. Their understanding stems from the fact that they were in at the beginning. Your confusion stems from coming in halfway.

We will only understand prayer if we start at the beginning – and that means starting with God. Most of us start too far along the line, in the middle of 'the action' – and we start with ourselves. The child does that. The world revolves around him. If he does not get what he wants, he yells or sulks. People are there to serve him, feed him, give him money to spend, love and help him. He is the centre of the world.

I had not realised how we think like this even nationally until travelling and seeing maps of the world published in the USA with the Americas central, published in Australia with Australia central, and in Britain with Britain central. We look out on the world from our centre.

In adult life we are still children in many ways, even though we may be more sophisticated about it! We are standing in a bus queue. There are fifteen people in the queue and we are the ninth. The bus is almost full. How many are we concerned should get on the bus – fifteen or nine?!

It is this attitude that can be reflected in prayer. In one sense it is fine that we should share our needs with our God. After all, we *are* his children by faith in Christ. So isn't it

3

natural that Jeremy prays about his new job or the exams he is facing; that Jill prays about her deep longing to be married; that Jonathan prays for snow for his winter sport's holiday; that Jean prays for the success of the operation to remove a cataract from her eye; that Joseph prays for protection as he sets out on a long and dangerous journey; that Janet prays for success as she sets out on a shopping expedition to get a new party dress? Yes, it *is* natural to pray about such things – as children sharing with our Father.

But it is not stage one. If we *start* there we get ourselves into all sorts of tangles and problems, which can result in loss of faith, and even despair. After all, asking for things to happen for his own benefit is the way the non-Christian uses prayer too.

The Air Force Padre meets a pilot walking across the tarmac. 'Do you pray?' asks the padre.

'Yes, of course!'

'Well, I've never seen you at my chapel services.'

'No, padre. I only pray when I'm flying – when I am on the ground I can cope.'

Typically, the non-Christian uses prayer to get what he wants – what will make his life easy and happy. God is almost a 'genie of the lamp' to be rubbed and called to do our bidding. 'Master,' says the genie to Aladdin, 'What is *your* will?' Then when the non-Christian doesn't get his answer he disposes of the genie. 'I prayed for my son to come back from the war. He didn't. So I no longer believe in God.' 'I prayed that my wife would be cured of cancer. She wasn't. I lost my faith in God.'

The Christian can easily imbibe a similar attitude. What then does he do if his prayer does not work out as he wants? If Jeremy does not get his new job, or fails his exams; if Jill remains single; if Jonathan finds the mildest winter on record when he reaches the Bernese Oberland – and almost no snow; if Jean's cataract operation is not a success; if Joseph breaks his car axle on a remote mountain road; if Janet comes back from the shops not having found one dress she likes?

Some Christians will tell you that the fault is in the way

you prayed – as if God would only answer if the right formula is used. On one of our European holidays we went to visit the cascade at Schaffhausen in Switzerland. As we came to the border from Germany we disposed of all our German coinage in buying petrol, because we were returning to England through France and would not need German currency again. Thirty minutes later we were parking in one of the designated car-parks by the cascade. There were warning signs that you needed Swiss francs to operate the release gate on leaving the car-park. We remembered that we had some coins left over from the previous year and so, when we left, we put the coins into the machine. The coins came out. The gate did not lift. We tried again; banged the machine. Still no result. By now a great number of vehicles had gathered behind us. There was some vigorous talking in German. They tried the coins. Same result. Suddenly, to our deep embarrassment, one German noticed that we were using French francs! More embarrassment – the machine only worked on German marks or Swiss francs. We had disposed of all our German ones. We had not broken any Swiss notes. The German paid for us – and the 40-car queue got out of the car-park! But God is not like that. He does not decline to respond unless we put in the right prayer 'coin'. He is not a heathen God demanding a particular incantation of words or actions before he will answer (like the woman who said to me, 'Your niece will not recover until you lay hands on her'). He is our heavenly father, dealing with us as his children. It is a family relationship. So the problems encountered by Jeremy, Jill and the others are not to be explained away by saying they didn't pray properly.

What about incidents in the Bible? Here again we see the same variety of answers to prayer that we observe in our lives. Here are a few examples:

The son of Paul's sister hears of an ambush to kill Paul. Paul avoids the ambush and lives. (Acts 23)	Stephen is arrested, and, after preaching, is stoned to death. (Acts 7)

Peter is miraculously delivered from prison by the angel of the Lord, while others were praying for him.
(Acts 12)

John the Baptist is kept in prison, then beheaded, and his head brought in on a platter.
(Mark 6)

The lame man at the temple is healed instantly by Peter, and walks and leaps.
(Acts 3)

Epaphroditus, a great servant of God, has a long illness, and comes near to death.
(Phil. 2.26)

A boy falls asleep during Paul's sermon, falls from the third floor, is taken up for dead. Paul raises him to life.
(Acts 20)

Trophimus is so ill that Paul actually has to leave him behind at Miletus.
(2 Tim. 4.20)

James says, 'The prayer of faith will save the sick.'
(James 5)

Timothy is told to take a little wine for his stomach and his frequent ailments.
(I Tim. 5.23)

The storm on the lake is stopped at the command of Jesus and the boat comes safely to shore.
(Mark 6)

The storm on the Mediterranean is allowed to run its full course. The boat is wrecked, but all are saved.
(Acts 27)

We are aware of this variation in our lives and in the lives of those close to us. The telephone rings. 'I'm terribly sorry to tell you that Ruth has contracted acute lymphoblastic leukaemia.' Ruth was then fifteen – one of our nieces – a delightful Christian girl soon to take her 'O' level examinations. Leukaemia! One's blood ran cold. This young life with so much potential for Christ – and now, leukaemia. The bump had been spotted rapidly, diagnosed accurately and immediately. Ruth was taken into hospital. Was there any hope? I will mention some more details later in the book, but suffice it to say here that her family (who are Christians) prayed with unswerving faith; her home church

6

(Chatsworth Baptist Church in South London) began regular and realistic times of special prayer; we and many others prayed fervently. In God's mercy the treatment, timings, 'co-incidences' worked together. Ruth came through, with her faith and witness radiant, and seeming to want to live twice as much for Jesus Christ as before. That was more than ten years ago. Ruth became a medical student at the hospital where she was treated and married another medic. Dr Ruth sees her life given back to her by God. Yes, we believe in God's healing in answer to prayer. But at the same time, in the same church, another became seriously ill – similar age, faith, praying family, praying church. He too was carried to God on the stretcher of faith-prayer. He died. Why? 'Why?' said their beloved pastor, Andrew McKie, 'in the same church, with the same love and prayer – one lives, one dies?'

I sit at the back of a special meeting. We are marking the long life and ministry of one of God's long-serving saints who has been out on the mission-field for a lifetime and is now going on witnessing for Christ at home – still going strong at ninety! Then comes news from Manorom Hospital in Thailand of a terrible car crash – an accident on the way to a picnic in which several brilliant young surgeons, doctors, wives and children – all in Thailand to serve Christ – were suddenly killed – snatched from the world with a harshness that numbed one's heart. Why? Why such loss? Why such devastation to the work at Manorom? And why should some servants of God live on this earth into their nineties and others depart so soon?

There are two girls – young ladies. They are both delightful Christians, lovable, witty, intelligent. They both long to get married and pray about it even though they have faced up to the possibility of remaining single in a sensible way. Suddenly one is swept off her feet by a proposal that leaves her reeling. The young man is marvellous. He has proposed to her. She hardly has enough breath to say 'yes!' The marriage is marvellous. Yet the other girl remains single for life, in spite of being an equally wonderful person and potentially an equally good wife.

Several young people are searching for accommodation.

7

They pray. Suddenly one finds 'the perfect place.' He gives thanks in the prayer gathering and exudes his joy all over the place. The others feel downcast. They are still searching and still praying.

All these examples end up in problems *if* we start with ourselves as the centre and not with God at the centre. If God is there to do our bidding, then we will discard him if he 'doesn't work.' Of course we would not put it as bluntly as that, but it *is* what we feel. So a girl asks to see me after a service. We sit in a pew together.

'What's wrong?' I ask.

'God doesn't keep his promises.'

'What do you mean?'

'God doesn't keep his promises,' she repeated.

I ventured a direct approach: 'What you mean, I think, is that you have asked God for a husband and yet you remain single.' I was on target. Her view of prayer was 'the genie of the lamp' – 'ask what you will, believing, and you will receive it.' She had asked for a husband. She hadn't received. No other possibilities or factors are allowed in this simplistic approach. God is to blame. He scores nil and is to be discarded.

Here is a married couple – happy and apparently Christian, involved in the life of the church. The wife contracts cancer. The husband is desperate. He asks for prayer, finds out about faith healers and is prepared to try anything. The situation worsens. The cancer is rampant. There is special prayer and laying on of hands. The cancer is advanced. It is a moment to face up to it, to share what time is left of life together. But instead, there is a frenetic insistence that God is going to heal. God *must* heal. God cannot let his wife suffer and die. The wife dies. The reaction is sadly predictable. The husband turns on God in hate and cuts himself off from the one who could surround him in love – and separates himself from his believing partner who is now with the Lord. Many people are hurt. Yet all because the prayer of the man started from self – to make God do his will.

We will never sort out the privileges and problems of prayer when *we* are at the centre.

8

So 'let's start at the very beginning – it's a very good place to start!' The beginning is God.

We need a God-centred perspective. The world revolves around *God*, not around me. There are more than four thousand million people in the world and you and I are just two of them. We will only begin to understand ourselves when we see ourselves as a tiny part of the human race – God's creation – with God over all.

There are millions of believing Christians in the world and you and I are just two of them. We will only begin to understand ourselves as Christians when we see ourselves as a tiny part of the Body of Christ.

We need a God-centred trust. If we walk around a vast farming area in Norfolk or Ohio we may find it difficult to understand why one field is cultivated, another lying fallow, another being used for hay. If I start with my limited understanding of farming, I shall be puzzled. I must start instead with the farmer. What is his overall purpose – why is there life in one field and nothing happening in another? He knows. It is in his plan. I may not comprehend it, but I know the farmer and I am therefore confident that he knows best. I must trust him.

So that is where we must start concerning prayer. We must start with the Lord over all, the Creator, Sustainer, the Head of the Body, the Lord of the Church, the Divine Farmer – in whose world, body, church, and harvest field we find ourselves.

'Let's start at the person who *is* the Beginning –
He is the only good place to start....'

2 BUILDING THE FOUNDATIONS:

First – Faith in God as God

It is one thing to say 'I'll start with God,' but how do we spell that out? How do we establish understanding and convictions that will stand the test of anything life throws at us in future years? There are five foundations to build. The first, which we will look at in this chapter, is faith in God as God. Faith must lay hold of God, whatever the circumstances. It has to be learnt when skies are blue but will be proved when the clouds come. It is out of long-established conviction that Paul can write to Timothy from prison (II Timothy 1.12): 'I am not ashamed, for I know *whom* I have believed (in whom I trusted) and I am sure that he is able to guard until that day what has been entrusted to me.' It is not the imprisonment that fills Paul's mind but the Lord and his absolute faithfulness. Similarly, in the middle of the raging storm in the Mediterranean Paul is assured by God that all will be saved and so he can shout out the words across the deck in the teeth of the wind: 'I believe God that it will be exactly as I have been told.'

So often the Psalmist is bewildered by events. He cannot explain them. Suffering seems to continue; the heathen prosper; he feels forsaken and a long way from God. Yet whenever he feels like this he fights back to the foundation conviction: 'Who is a rock except our God?' (Ps.18) and 'though the earth trembles, the mountains shake and the waters roar we will not fear' because 'God is our refuge and strength, a very present help in trouble' (Psalm 46). So often we need to stop, put the brakes on, let the dust settle and get perspective restored. Events overwhelm us, crashing in on us one after the other like the waves on the sea-shore. God wants us to pause, in the quiet. He says: 'Be still, and know that I am God.' Get your perspective restored day after day. He is God and you belong to him. Everything else is secondary to that wonderful fact. Let it grip you, flood your heart. Leap down the street in its joy. The Lord is God. The Lord is God! And we belong to him for ever.

This is what grips the heart of Habakkuk (3.17) in those amazing words of testimony: 'Though the fig tree does not blossom, nor fruit be on the vines, the produce of the olive fail, and the fields yield no food, the flock be cut off from the fold and there be no herd in the stalls, yet I will rejoice in the Lord!'

To city dwellers the cutting force of that testimony is softened – so let's put it into a modern city equivalent: 'Though my business schemes fail, profits become losses, I lose my job, my bank balance dwindles to nothing, and I cannot see where I am going to get another job or how I'm going to be able to support my family, yet I will rejoice in the Lord!' He trusts God – even when the picture is so black. Can I do that? Could I have done that in the face of torture and murder in Cambodia? Could I do that in the waterless deserts around the Red Sea where drought goes on and on? Am I, in my present circumstances, able to home in on to God every time and to trust him, even when I do not understand why events are happening to me?

God's honours board of faith in Hebrews 11 hit me vividly a few years ago. Up till then I had not seen the full orbit of walking by faith. The phrase 'The just shall live by faith' (or 'my righteous one shall live by faith') had been to me a battle-cry of salvation – of being right with God through faith alone. But in Hebrews 10.38 I discovered it to be referring to the continuing Christian life as well. No longer could I feel that faith was a milestone passed when I came to Christ as my Saviour. It was now to challenge my thinking, daring, acting and pioneering for Christ – not receiving Christ and then living life as comfortably as possible but receiving Christ and going on and on with him at the centre. Hebrews 11 gives four categories of faith worked out in practice, faith without which 'it is impossible to please him.' (verse 6)

1 WORTHSHIP FAITH

Faith puts God at the centre of our lives because he is

worthy of all our honour and adoration. He is worth more to us than any human being, any thing or being in the whole universe. Abel expresses that with simple significance when he and Cain are to bring offerings to God. Cain brings 'of the fruit of the ground' but Abel brings 'of the firstlings of his flock and of their fat portions'. You can imagine Cain going out to his gardening area and picking a few things at random so that he could make some sort of offering. But Abel picks the best – he chooses the firstling of the flock and the fat portions. For him only the best is good enough for God. His giving reflects his 'worthship faith.'

Almost nothing sorts out Christian integrity and love for the Lord so quickly as giving. How do we give on a Sunday? Are we like Cain – giving something but without much thought or sacrifice, giving because we can hardly pass the offering plate by? Or are we like Abel – loving God, longing to see His work go forward, expressing this in thought – through proportionate giving and often in overflowing love-gifts as well. Of course, giving is not confined to a Sunday nor to Christian objectives but giving is a reliable indicator of whether you have God 'at the centre.'

2 EXPLOIT FAITH

What we might call 'exploit faith' occupies the majority of Hebrews 11. It is exciting to recall the great faith of Noah, Abraham, and Moses. They dared and obeyed. They saw the floods of judgement, the making of a nation, the deliverance from Egypt, the crossing of the Red Sea and so much more. It fires our blood to read of what happened. The film-makers have been fascinated too and have produced their epics. Applying the lessons of 'exploit faith' is also exciting in the present day. The same God is our God today and when he leads his people into ventures of faith then exciting times follow and great is the testimony to his power and enabling. I'm an enthusiastic 'exploit' man, as I have outlined in *Moses and the Venture of Faith*,* and, since writing that book, have had the joy of seeing countless

*(*The Moses Principle* published by Harold Shaw in the USA)

12

ventures elsewhere proving God to be the same God. Exploits for God, when God calls and man obeys, are a further indicator that we have 'God at the centre.'

3 DELIVERANCE FAITH

Then in verses 33-35 we have mentioned that element of faith in which special things happen – times when people have been specially strengthened for battle, or, as for Daniel, when the mouths of the lions have been stopped. Even resurrection from the dead is mentioned here. We love to see such things happening. What a joy it is to us when we see a friend suddenly healed, or someone released from a communist prison-camp, or a visa granted for a missionary at the last minute after months of applying, or a friend finding somewhere to live just in time. Such matters are the theme of the church's prayer-gathering, of the sharing with other friends in prayer, and we all get to share in the praising when deliverance happens in answer to faith. There are endless paper-back books telling the stories of deliverance faith and they are avidly consumed. We expect God to be involved in our daily lives and so 'deliverance faith' is a third indicator that we have 'God at the centre.'

4 DISASTER FAITH

Yet there is another category of faith in this chapter – a category that is often omitted. 'Disaster' faith is not really the best title for it, as it is as much triumph as disaster. Look at verse 36. Here are those who suffered mocking, scourging, chains, imprisonment. They were stoned, sawn in two, killed with the sword; they went about in skins of sheep and goats, destitute, afflicted, ill-treated – of whom the world was not worthy. By *faith*? Yes, by faith! No exploit to recall years later. No deliverance to give praise for in the prayer gathering. Instead, persecution to death, suffering and torture – what the world would call 'disaster.' Their experiences are not mentioned by those who would want us to believe that if we have enough faith we can be healed or delivered from anything. For here in Hebrews 11 we have faith at its highest – faith that holds on to the living God when there is no light in the darkness, no relief from the agony and healing of the pain. When men and women go on believing in the Lord in spite of such circumstances, their faith is faith indeed! Millions have demonstrated such faith, as they have been murdered simply for professing Christ, as they have spent long years in Siberian labour camps because they spoke up for Christ and truth, as they have been incarcerated in the body-packed cells of death camps under some insanely evil regime. Yet they believed, like their Saviour before them on the cross. They believed in God. There was no doubt at all that they had 'God at the centre.'

If we are to understand prayer we must start by building this first foundation – the foundation of the centrality of God in our lives. Our faith – worthship faith, exploit faith, deliverance faith, 'disaster' faith – must hold on to him whatever happens and even when we cannot understand or explain. Of such faith, William Barclay said: 'Obstacles will not daunt it, delays will not depress it, discouragement will not take its hope away.'

3 THE CHARACTER OF GOD

The second foundation to be built in our lives before we can approach the question of prayer is the character of God. We have just said that faith has to hold on to God even when it does not understand what is happening. That 'holding on' is much more assured when we know more about the God on to whom we are holding. We will also learn when not 'to hold on,' when repentance is needed and not petition, when correction of life is a prerequisite of God hearing our prayers.

When you think about it, it is amazing that people can live in total disregard of God – disobeying his laws, not keeping his ways – yet thinking that they can pray to him for help as soon as trouble comes. God is hardly personal to them. Rather, he is a distant prayer-receiver whom they operate with their on/off switch, and they may even select which religious or denominational channel to use! How far that is from the reality of prayer, in its personal relationship with the Lord and in its atmosphere of love, trust and obedience.

Yet Christians, too, can devalue the character of God in prayer. It was Sunday morning. The service was over and a committed Christian girl asked to see me. She was obviously upset. 'I have been praying for an answer all this week and haven't received one,' she blurted out. The matter was clearly urgent. I asked her to explain. Her sister had just had a baby in Canada and she wanted to go and visit her. In a few months' time her years in England would be ending in any case and she would be returning permanently to Canada. She wanted to make this quick visit now. A friend of hers had just flown over from Canada on a cheap return air flight but did not intend to return (at the time it was cheaper to get such a return ticket than a single!). So here was the chance to use her friend's ticket. Then she could get a cheap return ticket herself for her last few months back in England. Of course, it meant assuming her friend's identity and borrowing the passport, but they looked alike. So she had been praying about this all the week, and God had not answered! Because of her emotional involvement in wanting to see the baby it took some time to help her see that you cannot plan something contrary to the character of God and expect him to answer your prayer. We resolved that she would approach the airline to see if there was any legal way of transferring the ticket. There wasn't. She did not go. But she learnt a lesson for a lifetime that prayer cannot be effective if it is against the character of God. He is righteous.

Here are a delightful fellow and girl. They have a guidance problem and come to seek advice. They are both involved in leadership responsibilities within the church. Then I discover from their conversation that they are sleeping together, though unmarried. They think nothing of it – 'everybody's doing it.' I seek to show them the deep value God puts upon the beauty and exclusiveness of sexual relationship, how it is the climax of commitment and not a cheap forerunner. But particularly, in the light of why they had come to see me, I try to show them that you cannot sin deliberately and consciously against God's law and at the same time come to God expecting guidance and answers to prayer. God is not a machine. He is personal. His character has been shown to us. He is holy.

In the collapse of Samaria and the fall of Jerusalem in Old Testament history the cause lay not in mightier armies from outside, but in moral collapse from within. The Lord tells his people how he hates their feasts and their acts of worship because they are living with cruelty, lust, oppression of the poor, and self-centredness that sickens his heart. It is a basic fact for us all to grasp clearly. We cannot expect God to answer our prayers if we are deliberately living without love and obedience to him. The cause of unanswered prayer lies too often in *us*.

There are many other aspects of the character of God which challenge, strengthen or enrich our praying, but none so much as the covenant love of God. The great Hebrew word *hesed* is the anchor word of the Old

Testament. Translated variously as 'mercy' or 'steadfast love' it is *the* word to which the believer is to cling, the word to which he beats his path through the thickest jungle of despair, the word to which he climbs from the lowest depths of depression. Israel had been born in covenant love. As the solemn promises were made and the blood shed, God took these people as *his* people, as his beloved. That Israel and Judah presumed on that covenant love, taking it for granted, oblivious so often to its moral demands, did not alter the love itself. That God pleaded for response to his covenant love instead of endless and meaningless ritual sacrifices is vividly expressed in Hosea 6.6 and in the startling 'parable-picture' of the whole book of Hosea. So when the nation falls to the invader and is carried off into captivity, despair finding its outward expression in hanging the harps on the willow trees, the prophets focus on the only rock of hope that remained unmoved: the covenant love of God. In spite of all the misery and shame, they lay hold of the unshakable truth: 'The steadfast love of the Lord never ceases. His mercies never come to an end; they are new every morning; great is thy faithfulness.' (Lamentations 3 v. 23)

From there the picture of a 'new covenant' began to emerge – a personal covenant, but still of covenant love. For us this came to its glorious fruition in the Cross of Jesus Christ. When Jesus himself took the bread and wine, symbols of his body and blood, at the Last Supper, he said, 'This is the new covenant in my blood.' It is into this eternal covenant of love that we have entered by faith in Christ and it is on the unmovable rock of that covenant love that we must set our feet forever. The Holy Spirit makes it not just a mental acceptance but an inward experience. God's love (that is, the understanding of God's love for us in Christ) 'has been poured into our hearts through the Holy Spirit which has been given to us.' (Romans 5.5) It is part of the 'honeymoon experience' when we first come to personal faith – especially when that point comes clearly rather than gradually. How often a new believer has literally wanted to leap for joy with the wonder of it all and the overflowing sense of the love of the Lord. One of the most popular jobs in the church to which I belong is the care of those who have just come to faith – popular, because week by week they are alongside people in the first wonder of the covenant love of God. It is for so many a 'pouring into the heart' or 'flooding of the heart' with God's love by the Holy Spirit.

Yet, as we go on in the Christian life we do not live in a constant honeymoon, even though we often revel in the special touches of his love along the way. Instead, we go deeper into the effect of that covenant love on the whole of living. So Romans 5 moves through to Romans 8. Here are the realities of life in a sinful world – trouble, hardship, persecution, famine, nakedness, danger or 'sword.' If we want prayer to bring us a trouble-free life we are in difficulties. There is no promise here of escape, or of any of these things being removed. Instead there is the promise that none of these things – *none* of them – can separate us from the love of Christ. This is the key to triumphant living as a Christian – the grasp of the unchanging love that holds us, always.

This does not mean that we do not pray. We will pray when sickness strikes in our lives, when there is real hardship financially or in finding a job or coping as a widow with young children. We will pray when we are being mocked as a Christian, or imprisoned or sent to a labour-camp. We will pray in the face of danger, in time of war, in an accident or disaster. Sometimes we will give thanks for our Lord's evident intervention; at other times we will not see it in that way. In this sinful, fallen world Christians will be caught in the middle of war, epidemics or earthquakes like anybody else; they will be as subject to cardiac arrest or cancer. But the supreme over-riding factor for the Christian in any and every experience of life is that nothing – no powers or forces, no nuclear war or global holocaust, not even death itself – can separate us from the love of God in Christ Jesus our Lord. We must build this foundation securely so that, when troubles or problems come, we are not rocked.

Henry Venn – a great Christian of two hundred years ago – had to bear the death of his wife, leaving him five young children. He wrote: 'Did I not know the Lord to be mine, were I not certain his heart feels even more love for me than I am able to conceive, were not this evident to me, not by deduction and argument, but by consciousness, by his own light shining in my soul as the sun does upon my bodily eyes, into what a deplorable condition should I have been now cast.'

Henry Venn grasped hold of this immovable rock, but not everybody 'feels' the love of God as he did in that devastating time of his life. Others lose all sense of the love of God – they feel 'cold' and prayer seems impossible. Yet for them the only path of restoration will be via the same rock of covenant love.

When I was working in Manchester I learnt a lesson about this from our woman worker, Mary Hollinshead. An elderly member of the congregation – a lovely Christian woman, full of good works, caring for others and serving the Lord with joy and faithfulness – had gone into hospital with cancer. She was the last person you would expect to lose her faith, but that is what happened. Mary went to visit her and rapidly summed up the situation. 'I am not going to leave your bedside,' she said, 'until I hear you say again, from the heart, 'God is love.' It seemed tough treatment! Mary read to her from the Scriptures, talked with her, prayed with her. Eventually the elderly lady said from the heart, 'My God is love.' Later when she came out of hospital for a while she told the whole church: 'That was the turning point.' I have often followed Mary's example in ministering to others and am thankful for being shown the need to concentrate on that one foundation.

The character of God should be much in our minds as we pray, whether the sun is shining or the clouds are heavy. We will be encouraged in our whole approach to our Lord as we contemplate his wisdom, love, righteousness, goodness. George Müller – founder of an orphanage in Bristol in the nineteenth century – demonstrated a faith that God honoured in exciting and very practical ways. Many are the stories of food delivered 'at the last minute' or the exact sum of money required arriving in the morning post; but it is important to see the context of his faith. As he writes in his journal of a moment when they were down to the last £20 and 100 people needed to be fed, he does not begin by asking God for the money or food, but instead says: 'I was meditating on God's unchangeable love, power and wisdom, and turning all as I went to prayer.'

This, then, is the second foundation to be firmly laid as we approach the subject of prayer. The onslaught of 'Why should this happen to me? Why do I have to endure this suffering? Why doesn't God answer my prayer? Why doesn't God do what I ask?' will still come, but it will be met by an unshakeable conviction, an immovable foundation. Though I may not be able to explain why God does or does not seem to answer; though my feelings may become those of emptiness and desolation; yet I know God is love, that I am united to him for ever by covenant love, and that nothing can separate me from that eternal love. That foundation will stay secure – for ever.

4 THE PURPOSES OF GOD

The third foundation to be built concerns who is in control. The popular, non-Christian concept of prayer has ourselves 'in control' and God 'out there' to do our bidding when called upon. He is available to help us get what we want. We have our plans, our hopes, our purposes, and God is expected to fit in with them. If he doesn't, then we do not bother to pray any more.

We often sow the seeds of this approach in childhood. 'Now, children, we are having our sports day on Saturday, so let us pray that God will give us a sunny day.' The children pray in faith. 'It will be sunny on Saturday, Mummy, because we asked God for a sunny day.' 'What wonderful faith the children have,' say the adults to one another. But what do they mean by 'faith'? Is it not a faith in a God there to do our will? On Saturday the day dawns with a blue sky. It is a beautiful sunny day and apart from some sunburn the sports event goes splendidly. 'We prayed. God has given us this sunny day. Now let us thank God.' The incident is over. Similar incidents will occur and if things do not work out as prayed for – rain instead of sun, failure instead of success – it will be explained away with 'the farmers needed rain.' However, because the prayers originally prayed did not take that possibility into account the children will see prayer as a manipulating of God to their wants. As life goes on, this view of prayer begins to get shaken.

I am sitting in a funeral car on the way to the cemetery. I have only been ordained a few weeks and I am new to funeral 'reactions' in that city parish. It is a tragic situation – the death of a child. 'It makes yer think,' says the grandmother.

'What do you mean?' I asked in my naivety.

'Whether there's a God at all,' she said.

Here was the 'God-not-doing-what-we-asked' attitude.

21

Later in my ministry I became used to such remarks. Often they were accompanied by 'I lost my faith'. 'I prayed for my husband to come back safe from the war and he was killed ... I lost my faith.' 'I prayed for my child to be protected every day and yet she had that accident on her bicycle ... I lost my faith.' Gently one has to say, 'That sort of "faith" needs to be lost. It isn't Christian faith.'

Yet how far do we let that sort of thinking creep into our praying even as Christians?

We need deliberately and constantly to re-affirm as Christians that the purposes of God are greater and more important than the purposes of man. In becoming a Christian, 'by one Spirit we were all baptised into one body.' (I Corinthians 12 . 13) As members of the body of Christ we have a part to play in fulfilling the purposes of the head. Our roles will vary but, together with the other members, we serve Christ as Lord. Our greatest task and privilege in life is in fulfilling his purposes for us and through us. Once this vision has filled our hearts and minds we put our own purposes, wants and needs into second place.

Jesus expressed this truth in a slightly different manner in his Sermon on the Mount. 'Do not worry about your life, what you will eat or drink; or about your body, what you will wear. Is not life more than food, and the body more than clothing? ... These are the things the pagans are always concerned about. Your Father in heaven knows that you need them all. But seek *first* his kingdom and his righteousness, and all these things shall be yours as well.' (Matthew 6 . 25-33) So it isn't that our heavenly Father is unconcerned about the practical things – his care is that of a Father. But the purposes of his kingdom matter more and they are to matter more to us in our praying and living. Thus, our prayer requests must be submitted to the over-riding purposes of our God, who sees the end from the beginning.

Let's see the same principle in a human picture. As a family we have been on holiday to Switzerland, camping in our vehicle and revelling together in the wonderful scenery. Now we are motoring back through France. It is around midday and we are all feeling hungry. Ahead of us is a place where we could pull the car off the road under the shade of trees and beside a meadow and stream. 'Just the place for a picnic, Dad, let's stop!' Now imagine my answer: a warm 'yes' and a swinging of the car wheel into the selected spot? Certainly as a father I would be delighted to do so and for us all to enjoy the picnic together in that lovely place. So if I can, I will say 'yes'. But I may have to say 'no', in spite of the chorus of dismay from the back of the car. I will not enjoy saying 'no'. Nor will I enjoy the thought of everyone getting hungrier (although some biscuits distributed around the car may help for a while). My 'no' will only be because of a more important purpose – catching the boat at Calais.

There must be so many times when we pray to our heavenly Father about something affecting our lives or the lives of others and the Father says, 'Yes, of course, let's enjoy this together.' We rejoice in the answer to prayer, the sense of his presence and the blessings all round. Yet there will be the times when some greater purpose has to be the deciding factor and when our request must be put on one side or its answer delayed.

Zechariah and Elizabeth learnt this lesson in Luke 1. Their longing for a child must often have been on their lips in prayer. There was nothing in them to prevent their prayer being answered – they 'were both righteous before God, walking in all the commandments and ordinances of the Lord blameless.' The explanation for the delay was that God had chosen Elizabeth to bear John the Baptist as a son. The timing of John's birth was all-important. He was a vital part of the greater purposes of the Lord.

It seems too that at different points in our lives or in the development of a church or Christian work, God may alter his ways of answering prayer in order to train us, mature us or make us concentrate on different aspects of his work. He does this in the ministry of Jesus. Healing miracles abound – signs of who he is – up to the acclamation 'You are the Christ.' Then they become very rare. Jesus turns his attention to teaching the disciples and is far less involved in public preaching and healings.

People today who expect particular miracles to happen all the time to demonstrate the power of God seem to overlook that changing pattern in the gospels. The Lord has his purposes and if we really want to follow his we will be sensitive to his leading and his changes of emphasis in our lives and work. It is the same with his gifts to us. They are to enable us to serve and it seems likely that some gifts will be just for a time and others for life – as it suits the head of the body. The lesson in our lives and in our churches is not to decide God's purposes in advance, or to assume that what he purposed to do through a sequence of events ten years ago he will purpose to do through a similar sequence today. Prayer seeks and submits to his purposes.

When I was first ordained I was heavily involved in work amongst youth and children. In establishing the work amongst a lively bunch of 10-12 year olds I planned to take them away for a holiday, hiring a converted railway coach situated at the end of a quiet branch line by the sea. I was particularly pleased with the arrangements and when they were finally clinched across the telephone I raced through to the kitchen to tell my wife, leapt in the air for joy and more-or-less knocked myself out by hitting the doorpost with my head! However, I was then to receive a second blow. My vicar said, 'You can't take them there – you must not have these boys staying near a railway track – it is too dangerous.' I was annoyed, disappointed, hurt and generally downcast. However, the result was that I took them instead to a houseparty-camp run by a national Christian organisation, which was superb. What the boys received in every way was so much better than what I could have done for them, and it began an association with those camps for many years to come. The vicar's 'old-fashioned ideas' turned out to be a part of the Lord's greater purposes.

Is this not also true in the delicate matter of singleness and marriage? I think of some of my friends in the ministry who are single. Certainly some could never fulfil the important ministry to which they have been called if they were married. That may be because of constant worldwide travel, or of special Christian attributes, skills or insights

24

which demand much time in developing for the benefit of the wider Church. On the other hand, there are ministries of Christain leadership that would lose a great deal if they were not by married people – mine is one of them. Of course, it is not as obvious as that for many, but where a person has accepted, say, singleness positively and dedicated it to the Lord's purposes it usually strengthens his character and makes him a better fellow-worker for Christ.

Sometimes we have too narrow a vision to understand the purposes of God. When I was in my late teens I was a sea cadet, prior to conscription into the Army. I spent a week at 'camp' in Londonderry, Northern Ireland. On one of the days we went out on a destroyer for submarine-hunting in the Irish Sea. It was rather like a sophisticated version of the 'cops and robbers' games we played as children. There were several destroyers involved in 'the games.' We began by dropping bouys into the Irish Sea over a wide area. Attached to these bouys were radio transmitters. The destroyers sounded to the sea-bed below them, listening for sounds of the submarines in their area, but that was all they could do, apart from keeping tuned in to an aeroplane overhead. Only the 'plane had the receiving equipment to hear from all those little transmitting bouys. When eventually the 'plane heard the submarine it gave the position and the first destroyer to reach the spot was the winner. I can still remember feeling the comparative helplessness of the destroyers, only able to discern their piece of the ocean, and their dependence on the 'plane above that could see the whole picture. It has been a picture of guidance to me ever since. I may discern correctly the town, church, work-place, contacts and needs around me, but it is one small part of the Lord's vast universe. He can see it all – the needs in India, Africa or the USA as well. He can see inside the walls of prisons or New York skyscrapers or English suburban houses. He knows us through and through, with all our potential, talents and weaknesses. No-one else can more accurately fit me into God's purposes than God Himself!

As William Cowper put it:

> Deep in unfathomable mines
> Of never-failing skill,
> He treasures up his bright designs
> And works his sovereign will.
>
> His purposes will ripen fast
> Unfolding every hour;
> The bud may have a bitter taste
> But sweet will be the flower.
>
> Blind unbelief is sure to err
> And scan his work in vain;
> God is his own interpreter
> And he will make it plain.

Of course, as Cowper well knew, we do not always understand – at least, not at first. Peter, weeping his heart out at his denial of Jesus, was not likely to understand that the denial had been permitted by Jesus because out of the ashes of failure would rise a Peter of new humility and power, who later would write from the heart to his fellow-Christians: 'Humble yourselves therefore under the mighty hand of God, that in due time he may exalt you.' (I Peter 5.6)

Job had to learn the lesson the hard way. We sympathize with all he suffered, but then he starts to dispute with God, basing his arguments on his own fixed ideas about sin and suffering. Suddenly the boot is on the other foot. No longer is it Job questioning God but God questioning Job – 'Where were you when I laid the foundations of the earth?' And then Job gets things straight: 'I know that you can do all things, and that no purpose of yours can be thwarted. I have uttered what I did not understand, things too wonderful for me, which I did not know. . . . ' There was so much more than Job could have understood because it was beyond the human scene – Satan being permitted to prove Job.

The whole dimension of the spiritual battle, of the

wrestling with principalities and powers, of the global plans and purposes of our Lord, makes us marvel that we have a part to play at all! But we have, as members of his body. So, though we may often wish we could have the curtain lifted occasionally, like Elisha's servant in II Kings 6, and see that 'those who are with us are more than those with them,' we must be prepared to accept his purposes by faith. He will not be thwarted. He is 'working his purpose out as year succeeds to year.'

So this is the third foundation to lay if we are to understand prayer. We must accept gladly that, much as our heavenly Father encourages us to bring everything to him in prayer, and much as he loves to answer and bless, we are to seek first his kingdom and desire first his purposes.

5   THE WAYS OF GOD

The fourth foundation to be built is that of openness to the ways of the Lord.

Within our human families we often assume ways of doing things as if they were the norm for everyone and we are surprised to find that in other families they have different standards – in eating, for example – perhaps more informal than ours, or more formal with an evening meal at a set time and everybody 'dressed up.' When we visit other countries we often find bigger differences. The Britisher seems odd to the American when he uses knife and fork together. The American seems odd to the Britisher for cutting food up with his knife, then laying down the knife and picking up the fork to eat it with. When at a high-class restaurant in Los Angeles the waiter came round to ask whether I wanted a 'dawgy-bag' for 'left-overs' I couldn't believe it! A Christian girl came from Germany to England as an 'au pair'. The Christian family with whom she lived was shocked when she announced on the Sunday afternoon that she was going out to the cinema. 'But we don't do that on a Sunday,' said her hostess. Later in the afternoon the girl entered the lounge and saw her hostess knitting. Now she was shocked. 'But we don't do that on a Sunday in Germany.' They both laughed. How often we confine what we call 'the right way' or 'the wrong way' to what we are used to doing.

We can do exactly the same with God about the ways of answering prayer. We can pray for something to happen and at the same time have a mental picture of how God could – or should! – answer. When I was facing up to God's call to the ministry I knew that there was to be a special weekend at our church about vocation and ministry, in the first part of January. I had already been wakened to the call and had been praying for confirmation. This, I resolved, would be the weekend that God would make his way clear.

So I went to all the meetings and services expectantly. At the end of the Sunday evening nothing had happened. I was no further on. There had been no 'word from the Lord.' But around midnight when I opened a book of devotional readings and turned to the portion for the day I was startled to see that the text was Isaiah 6: 'Whom shall I send and who will go for us?' And the commentary on the text was like a live wire. It hit me with every sentence and made complete sense. I felt overwhelmed by the Lord and dropped to my knees with the words on my lips, 'Lord, here am I, send me.' His ways were completely different from mine.

That is our God. He told us so:

'My thoughts are not your thoughts,
Neither are your ways my ways, says the Lord.
For as the heavens are higher than the earth,
So are my ways higher than your ways
And my thoughts than your thoughts.'

(Isaiah 55 8)

That is how God acted in Old Testament history: the way in which he delivered his people from slavery – provided food in the wilderness – chose the shepherd-boy David – taught his people in the exile and restored his people to Jerusalem.

But nothing could have been more of a surprise to the human race than his way of making our salvation possible. Who would have thought of the incarnation, the humble birth in a stable, the simple life-style of a carpenter, the death of the Cross, the resurrection, the gift of the Holy Spirit? That is our God. His ways go far beyond our thinking and expecting.

Our minds need constantly to re-learn this truth. We must not confine God's ways of answering prayer to what we expect or to what we think he can manage.

It was our God who raised up a heathen king – Cyrus – as agent of his purposes, even calling Cyrus his 'shepherd' and his 'anointed.' It was our God who did not preach a sermon to Elijah in the depths of spiritual depression but delivered him a cake baked on hot stones and a jar of water. It was our God who spoke to the same Elijah not in the dramatic accompaniments of the victory on Mount Carmel – not in the storm, earthquake or wind that seemed to 'go' with Elijah's character – but in the still small voice. It was our God who chose to answer the Roman Cornelius's prayer by dealing with the Jewish Peter about his view of the Gentiles and then by the repeat of Pentecost – the pouring out of the Holy Spirit as it had happened to the Apostles 'in the beginning.' It was our God who answered the urgent and earnest prayer of the church for Peter in prison by bringing him out of that prison in a miraculous way, so that not even those who were praying could believe it. It was our God who blinded the great Saul on the Damascus road and used a 'nobody' – Ananias – to be his messenger and agent at that marvellous moment. It was our God who blocked Paul's plans across Asia Minor until he ended up in Troas and was then called to Macedonia and Europe. When God's people pray God's answers are often a complete surprise.

So down through the centuries of Christian history hundreds of thousands of such incidents have taken place. In every generation the Lord has answered prayer in *his* ways. If I picked but one it would be the lovely story of Billy Bray, the Cornish evangelist in the early nineteenth century, and his need of a pulpit for a chapel he was building. Seeing an old three-cornered cupboard in an auction sale he 'knew it was the very thing' for making into a pulpit. He went in. He had no money, of course! However, an enquiry of what it might be sold for provided not only the estimate of 'six shillings' but the actual cash from the person he asked. Billy was all set to bid 'six shillings,' but when the time came he was stunned to find himself outbid by a farmer. Surely God had meant him to have it? He decided to follow the 'pulpit' on its journey to the farmer's house. There he witnessed the farmer's anger when it was found that the cupboard would not go through the door of the house. Faced with having to chop it up for firewood, the farmer was only too glad of Billy's offer of six shillings 'if the farmer would have the cupboard transported to the chapel.' Billy Bray was overjoyed. His heavenly Father had not only supplied the pulpit but had arranged for it to be delivered as well for his six shillings!

Billy Bray had learnt to keep his eyes open for God's hand in events. Tragically some Christians restrict God to a very narrow kind of guidance. A young man came to see me about going into the ministry. 'I feel a deep inward conviction,' he said, 'all the circumstances fit together; my friends all think it right. My minister does – I am just waiting for a word from the Lord.' By which he meant a Bible text. God's ways are higher than our ways.

We had been praying at our church for some time that a person imprisoned for many years without trial in an African country would be released. Various enquiries were made and letters written. Then one Sunday morning we 'happened' to pray during the service for that prisoner. A distinguished leader from another part of the world was there. He wrote to me a few weeks later saying that leaders in his country (a country which had particular links with that African country) did not believe the reports of the imprisonment. Could I send evidence? I was able to send ample evidence. A few weeks later the prisoner was released. God's ways are higher than our ways.

I mentioned earlier my niece Ruth. Soon after her leukaemia was diagnosed my wife and I went to pray with her parents. It had been difficult to fix a time for us all to meet but suddenly it was possible and we asked a friend to come in as 'child-sitter.' As we settled her in to the house and began to leave she asked us what was wrong with Ruth. We told her. She responded at once: 'But I work for the top specialist in leukaemia in the country – I am sure he would help.' We had not known this when we asked her to child-sit. He was indeed willing to help, but only if he would be welcomed by the specialist dealing with Ruth. It turned out that the specialist knew the great man personally and was more than happy to have his help. So he kindly made the journey and saw Ruth several times. His expert knowledge was a significant help in commending, advising and supporting the medical treatment. Mercifully, re- mission began. God's ways are higher than our ways.

At one time my wife, Myrtle, felt clearly called to missionary service but suddenly in an evening service God 'closed the door.' Had she been wrong in her earlier sense of call? Then she and I met. We fell in love; we married into the ministry. God's earlier call had prepared the way and Myrtle had been willing to do anything and go anywhere. That was a very necessary preparation for life in the ministry. He called us both independently. God's ways are higher than our ways.

We may often learn from other Christians and other churches who have faced similar problems and challenges to ours. Principles of faith and prayer will often be the same – but the ways of God's answering may be vastly different. Many churches have tackled building projects and have adopted many of the principles described in *Moses and the Venture of Faith.* (also published by Mowbray). Sometimes as I have seen the challenges they have faced, I have trembled. Yet when God calls his people out he is the faithful God who brings them through the impossible. It has been wonderful to see so many faith projects – and God dealing with each of them in his own way. God does not fit easily into books of methodology. His ways are higher than our ways.

So in prayer we learn to say 'Lord, your will be done.' It amazes me that some people will tell you that it shows lack of faith to tag 'if it be your will' on to a prayer. On the contrary, it is a mark of true faith, because faith is submission to the Lord and to his purposes and to his ways. What we want most is his will not ours. We do not want to persuade him to do *our* will.

Let us lay this fourth foundation firmly. With Moses, let us cry from the heart, 'Show me your ways.' Let us not confine God, or miss his answers and his blessing, because we are not open to his ways of responding. Let us trust him to work as he sees best. Then increasingly we shall echo Paul's words (Romans 11.33): 'O the depth of the riches and wisdom and knowledge of God! How unsearchable are his judgments and how inscrutable his ways!'

6   THE PROMISES OF GOD

The fifth foundation – the promises of God – is perhaps better thought of as a platform resting on the four foundations we have already considered. Our encouragement to come to God in prayer is because he has invited us to do so. He has reinforced that invitation with great promises of his readiness to hear and to answer. However, if we start with these promises as the foundation for prayer we get into difficulties.

Take John 15.7 for instance: 'If you abide in me, and my words abide in you, ask whatever you will, and it shall be done for you.' Anthony is 16, facing crucial exams at school. He is a Christian. He takes hold of this promise – 'ask whatever you will and it shall be done for you' – and asks for a high success rating in his exams. Is he right or wrong? Angela longs for a steady boy-friend, and then for marriage. She takes hold of this promise. She asks expectantly. Is she right or wrong? Graham is an evangelist. He prepares to speak at an evangelistic meeting. He takes hold of the promise. He asks for seven conversions at the meeting. Is he right or wrong?

Another promise is in Mark 11.23-24: 'Whoever says to this mountain, "Be taken up and cast into the sea,' and does not doubt in his heart, but believes what he says will come to pass, it will be done for him.' Patricia has a problem with asthma. It is difficult to cope with it and some of the attacks she gets, fighting for breath, are quite terrifying. Someone points her to this promise in Mark 11. She prays and claims the promise. Her asthma continues. She goes on praying and claiming the promise. Things remain the same. The person who pointed her to the verse tells her of someone fully delivered from asthma by claiming this promise and goes on to suggest that Patricia doesn't have enough faith. She must have more faith and when she has sufficient faith the 'mountain' of asthma will go. So when it goes on

Patricia feels a spiritual failure. Or is the promise of God not reliable?

These 'problems' only arise if we *start* with the promises. But when we stand on them as a platform supported by the foundations of faith in God as God, the character of God, the purposes of God and the ways of God, then the problems recede and the blessings come into focus.

Take the John 15.7 promise again. The context is of deep union with the Lord, as the branch in the vine. The whole atmosphere is of the Lord's centrality (he is the vine, we the branches), the character of God (judgment, v. 2 and v. 6; cleansing, v. 3; love, vv. 9-10), the purposes of God (to make us bearers of much fruit, vv. 2, 4, 5, 8; and for the Father thus to be glorified in us, v. 8) and the ways of God (removing dead branches, v. 2 and v. 6; and pruning fruit-bearing branches to produce more fruit, v. 2). The result in the Christian will be fullness of joy at being fruitfully used by the Lord. So, using John 15.7 to get exam passes, a husband, or a specific number of converts sounds oddly out of tune with the whole chapter. Clearly the person who really wants to be in tune with the chapter will be praying for ways to glorify the Lord more and to be more fruitful in his service. This must mean pruning, and pruning hurts while it is happening even if we can see the reasons for it later.

To press the point more sharply, if we really pray from the heart in terms of John 15.7 then we are openly saying to the Lord 'choose what way I can glorify you.' It may be his will to glorify himself through strengthening us to triumph in and over a lifetime's affliction, as so clearly and marvellously with Joni Eareckson. Think of the testimonies you have heard and the Christian lives you have seen. Some have been snatched from disaster and others have shone in the midst of pain. This is the Hebrews 11 pattern we saw earlier. With the four foundations underneath it, John 15.7 will not lead us astray but become a promise that we will dare to claim more and more. Dare? Yes! Because we will be wanting God's glory and fruit in our lives as he wills.

In Mark 11.22-24 we have a context involving the four foundations too. The disciples do not understand about the fig tree withering, with its relationship to the disobedient and fruitless Jewish nation. It goes beyond them and Jesus brings them back to trust in God even when they do not understand. The character of God comes into the picture with the attack on the commercialising of the temple – the turning of God's 'house of prayer' into a den of robbers. Later too, just after the promise, is the reminder that we must come to prayer in an attitude of forgiveness to others so that we can be cleansed and forgiven ourselves. The closer we come to the promise of verses 23 and 24 the more we see that it can only have meaning in the forwarding of the purposes of God, in the removing of blocks to the advance of his kingdom. To use it for our personal needs or healings presses it right out of context. But for all of us engaged in the spiritual battle, wrestling against principalities and powers, and all the forces of darkness – whether in the pioneer mission field, the inner city, the materialistically-sated suburbs or anywhere else – it is a promise to claim.

Alongside the prayer promises we need to take the great prayer ascription of Ephesians 3.20 – a text that has meant so much to me in my ministry and in ventures for the Lord: 'Now to him who by the power at work within us is able to do far more abundantly than all that we ask or think, to him be glory in the church and in Christ Jesus to all generations, for ever and ever. Amen'. It is the climax of Paul's prayer for the Ephesians – a prayer for spiritual growth and maturity, for spiritual strengh and power. How Paul longs for the church to increase in its impact – and his ascription shows that he sets no limits on what can happen.

The phrase 'far more abundantly' is vividly pictorial. It is basically the word *perisseuo* – 'to overflow.' Paul never thinks in terms of a dribble of blessing – always a fountain. But you can strengthen Greek words by adding prefixes to them. So he puts an *ek* in front of the word. That makes it a *great* overflowing – pouring over and flooding out. But even that is not enough for him. So he puts *huper* on the front of all that! Now the word is a Niagara Falls of blessing, with no limit to what God can do, except us: 'by the power at work *within us*' How often does a church or a Christian work miss out on what God can do because they do not trust him as God, because they limit their prayers to what they think he can cope with, and so live in spiritual puddles instead of under the cascade of the waterfall.

Look at the ascription again – this overflowing blessing is 'more than all that we ask or think.' Some years ago a petrol company was encouraging purchase of its petrol by offering 'Bizzy pens' (felt-tip pens) with its petrol. Our children were younger then, and their enthusiasm for this particular free offer dictated what brand of petrol we bought. We were travelling with our two boys to Scotland. Just across the Forth Bridge we came to a petrol station advertising Bizzy pens. Delight in the back of the car! We filled up. 'The pens please,' they asked.

'Och! They've all gone,' replied the attendant.

The boys were indignant. 'Can we put the petrol back?!'

Some days later we needed to fill up again. This time we were more careful. We asked first and the Scottish garage-owner carefully doled out one bizzy pen for each four gallons purchased. On our way home through England the Bizzy pen garages seemed few and far between. The petrol gauge was touching zero. The situation was tense! 'We'll have to stop at the next garage whatever the brand of petrol,' I said. There was reluctant agreement in the back of the car. We were climbing a long hill. Suddenly over the horizon there appeared the top of the petrol company's sign. Excitement grew. Gradually the pole beneath it came into view. Sure enough, there was the sign: 'Bizzy pens.' The boys were on their feet cheering. As soon as we pulled in they approached the pump attendant. 'How many Bizzy pens can we have?'

'As many as you like,' he said.

That was good enough for our lads, who staggered back to the car with arms full! That is *huper-ek-perisseuo* – super-overflowing more than you ask or think! That is our God. He is not a God who doles out one blessing for every four good deeds, or who runs out of blessings altogether, but a God who wants to see his church go forward praying, expecting, daring, believing, so that he can match that with his overflowing blessing – and the glory will be his.

So, if we are to understand prayer, we must *start with God*. We must lay firmly the foundations: of faith in God as God – God central, of the character of God in his holiness and love, of the purposes of God being worked out as year succeeds to year, of the ways of God in their rich and sometimes surprising variety. Next, we must build on to those foundations the great prayer promises. Then we must stand up and ascribe to him trust in his power and the desire for his glory – as the God who by the power at work within us is able to do far more abundantly than all that we ask or think – a *huper-ek-perisseuo* God! To him be glory in the church and in Christ Jesus to all generations, forever and ever. Amen!

SECTION TWO

APPROACH TO GOD

7 APPROACH TO GOD

– With Worship

How do we approach God before we come with our petitions?

There are many patterns for us to adopt in our approach to God, the best known possibly being A-C-T-S: adoration, confession, thanksgiving . . . and then, supplication. All of them put requests last; all of them begin with worship.

It is said that Dr R.A. Torrey found his experience transformed when he learned not only to pray and thank but to worship, to spend time not only asking but being 'occupied with God.' Many Christians do not start here – indeed they seldom truly worship the Lord. Take a church service. Some people enter the church one minute before, or even after, the start. They go through the various words, hymns and items; they give some attention to the sermon. Then they go out at the end and join in the hubbub of conversation about Billy's new girl-friend and Sheila's new car. But where is God in it all? Was there any sense of coming to meet with the living Lord, with wonder, awe and adoration and expectant of God's blessing, conviction or challenge? Would a stranger coming into the church have sensed that they were worshipping God? It is so easy for any of us to slide into this slipshod and irreverent facade of 'worship.' The same is too easily true of our personal prayer time. It can become a segment of our day, fitted in between all the other demands of the day, and its content a shopping list of requests without any real conscious entering into the presence of the Lord.

So what is worship?

Worship is, of course, 'worth-ship' – giving God the glory and honour which is due to him. At the same time it is an expression of our dependence upon him and our submission to him as Lord. Frequently in Scripture, worship is associated with falling down or kneeling. This was not confined to the Jews or to Christians. You will recall that the decree of King Nebuchadnezzar in Daniel 3.10 required everyone to 'fall down and worship the gold image.' It would have been natural for the Wise Men, when they came into the house where the child Jesus was, to 'fall down and worship.' When Satan tempted Jesus to submit to his 'authority' he took Jesus to a high mountain and showed him the kingdoms of the world and the glory of them and said, 'All these I will give you, if you fall down and worship me.' When Peter arrived at the house of Cornelius he was embarrassed by Cornelius kneeling down and worshipping him. This action expresses submission to the authority and superiority of another and as there is no greater authority in heaven and earth than the Lord's and no one superior to him, it is our duty and privilege to respond to the exhortation of Psalm 95: 'O come, let us worship and bow down, let us kneel before the Lord our Maker! For he is our God, and we are the people of his pasture, and the sheep of his hand.'

How do we worship?

Two important texts will guide us in our attitude to worship:
John 4.24 : 'God is spirit. And those who worship him must worship him in spirit and in truth.'
Romans 12:1 : 'I appeal to you, brethren, by the mercies of God, to present your bodies as a living sacrifice, holy and acceptable to God, which is your spiritual worship.'
Three areas of our beings are involved: our spirit, our mind (truth) and our body. Real worship will consciously involve all three.

(a) Spirit

When Jesus spoke to the woman at the well he knew that her 'worship' was a formal activity depending on what was done and how it was done. Jesus pressed her to the heart of worship. No form of service, however good, is worship – it is only the vehicle of worship. In Jesus Christ a new experience of spiritual worship was to be opened up by the Holy Spirit. Here men and women would be indwelt by the Holy Spirit and he would inspire, enlighten and empower from within. For all of us in Christ this is our privilege. We must therefore take time to become attuned to the Spirit of God within us as we approach the Lord. We cannot just charge into his presence and deliver our requests. We must come unhurried, asking the Holy Spirit to open our hearts. He will want to witness with our spirit that we are the children of God, he will want to glorify Jesus, he will want to take the things of God and open them to us, he will want to interpret spiritual truth to us, he will want to open the depths of our being in adoration and worship – often without words, or taking the words of Scripture or of hymns and releasing our hearts to make these our own expressions of worship. Whether on our own in daily devotion or in a church service or group worship, the Holy Spirit takes the parts and lifts us through them and above them in spiritual worship.

This spiritual dimension is eternal – it unites us with the whole of heaven. Hebrews 12.18-24 lifts the curtain for us. When we come to the Lord in worship, it says, we are coming to 'Mount Zion and to the city of the living God, the heavenly Jerusalem, and to innumerable angels in festal gathering, and to the assembly of the first-born who are enrolled in heaven, and to a judge who is God of all, and to the spirits of just men made perfect, and to Jesus, the mediator of the New Covenant.' Here we are, on our knees in our bedroom or sharing in the service on a Sunday, yet part of the vast family of God in heaven. We are citizens of heaven, in exile for the moment, but united by the Holy Spirit to the eternal family to which we belong. So we often say in the Communion Service: 'With angels and archangels and with all the company of heaven, we proclaim your great and glorious name; evermore praising you and saying: "Holy, holy, holy Lord, God of power and might, heaven and earth are full of your glory.'

(b) Mind

Jesus added the words 'and in truth' to what he said about worship in John 4.23. There was much error in the Samaritans' religion, as there was in the pharisaism of some of the Jews. Jesus was constantly exposing error and teaching the truth. In much of his teaching ministry he used parables and stories to illustrate, but he never watered down the truth itself. 'I am the way, the truth and the life,' he said. Men had to face up to that truth. In John 6.66, after his teaching about his body and blood, 'many of his disciples drew back and no longer went about with him.' Jesus asked the twelve: 'Will you also go away?' and Peter answered: 'Lord, to whom shall we go? You have the words of eternal life.' The truth divides. It also liberates: 'If you continue in my word, you are truly my disciples, and you will know the truth and the truth will make you free.' (John 8.31-32). The church from Pentecost onwards has sought to teach, spread and protect the truth of God. Mindless worship is contrary to the spirit of the New Testament and even those engaged in the 'ecstatic' worship of I Corinthians 14 were told: 'In thinking be mature' (verse 20).

Worship must therefore include the submission of our minds to the wisdom of God – to his thoughts, which are higher than our thoughts. Meditation on the Scriptures, with an open mind and prayerful attitude, is essential within our daily worship. Whether we follow a lectionary, or some other system of Bible reading, or create our own pattern, the object will be deeper than informing the mind. Notes and commentaries may help us but meditation is vital. What is the Lord saying to me in this passage this day? How am I to respond, to be a doer of the word and not a hearer only? What does the passage also show me of my God, his character and ways? Is there a particular truth or verse which so inspires me that I may take it on into my praying and on into the day?

The truth of God must also be a check on forms of worship. It cannot be acceptable to God if our attitude is 'anything goes.' He is to be worshipped 'in truth as well as in spirit,' and however much, for instance, we may want to share in friendship or dialogue with people of other religions, our commitment to the truth revealed to us by the Son of God will make us wary of multi-faith 'acts of worship'. Those of us belonging to churches with liturgical worship will also be concerned to have liturgies in accord with the truth of God and find it painful when expressions contrary to that truth are inserted. (Non-liturgical services often sit even more lightly to the truth!) In our own times of personal or corporate worship we must mean what we say to God; our minds must gladly affirm his revealed truth and submit to it; there should always be a measure of transformation of our lives by the renewing of our minds.

(c) *Body*

The body part of worship is the submission of my life to my Lord, putting myself entirely at my commanding officer's disposal and ready to do his will. My daily act of worship needs to include this surrender, laying my life at the Lord's feet for this day – for its work, its relaxation, its decisions, its conversations, its joys and sorrows, its opportunities for witness and service and for all its unknown content. This is a deliberate expression to God of submission to his purposes and his ways.

Such submission is movingly demonstrated by David in II Samuel 12.20. He gave himself to fasting and prayer for his child by Uriah's wife, Bathsheba, when it was ill. The child died. Then 'David arose from the earth and anointed himself and changed his clothes, and he went into the house of the Lord and *worshipped.*' Only then did he go to his own house to eat. The child's death was a judgement on David's appalling sin against Uriah, but David submitted and worshipped. I ask myself whether that world be how I would react to judgement or to a deep sorrow or bereavement. Is my life a life of worship?

There will be special times of worship, however, when I will want to dedicate my life anew to God's service, submitting to his overall direction and purpose. In such moments the whole course of life may be changed as God opens up new avenues of service, or calls me out of my present job to go for him to another part of the world. In such moments also he may confirm his present calling to stay where I am to continue serving him here. Either way, it involves the submission of my body in worship. Whoever we are we only have one life to live for God on this earth. Let it be the life he wants!

How do we prepare for corporate worship?

In corporate worship we are able to focus the attitude of worship and find inspiration from sharing together. At least, that is the idea – the reality may fall far short of that because of ourselves or because of the service itself.

Let us start with ourselves. If worship involves my spirit, mind and body, I cannot expect to 'click in' to a service of worship without preparation. People who get up late, rush to church, and arrive just before or after the service begins are in no state to worship the living God. The service will probably seem 'dead' or 'cold' and they may be critical afterwards of the contents of the service. But the fault is in themselves. Others have come out of church inspired and renewed, challenged and uplifted, because they took time to prepare themselves the night before or that morning before leaving home. They arrived in time to pray, to meditate, to look through the hymns set for the service so that later they could make them their own in worship. They came not 'to attend church' or 'to go to a service' but to meet with the Lord of heaven and earth and to worship him. Their anticipation and expectancy influenced their whole participation.

The other side is the service itself. Sometimes our anticipation and expectancy is sadly blunted and disappointed by a service that seems to be without preparation or meaningful leadership. It may happen to us when we are away from home and go on a Sunday to a local church. Sometimes it is a joy and delight – the Lord is uplifted and no-one could doubt that He is there; sometimes it is a deep sadness that there is so little life and reality. A considerable responsibility rests on all of us who lead services of worship. I was not trained to spend time planning services and it took a long while for it to dawn on me that when care and prayer went into planning a service, the Lord of the Church would bring it powerfully alive. In the church to which I belong we plan our preaching series months in advance, praying and discussing, seeking to sense the right balance of the 'preaching menu.' Then one, two or three hours a week are spent going through the hymn and psalm books, seeking the best material to support the preaching theme. Gradually the service takes on this thematic approach, even in the prayers, if that seems possible. The church family is urged to pray about the worship services – and does so together in the church prayer gathering. We all long that every service will be a special service – the Lord meeting with us in his particular way.

When there is preparation of worshippers and the service, there will be living worship. What a glorious experience it can be, to share in oneness with the Lord and one another in the service of Holy Communion. Then there are the occasions when we have the benefit of great music. Singing 'Crown him with many crowns' the other night with our church orchestra in full sound I felt I only needed the slightest push to float into glory! But that can be so with a squeaky harmonium or no music at all. The Lord may overwhelm us, as he did a young man who ran out of church because he felt the love of God so strongly he wanted to be alone. The Word of God may come powerfully to our minds and souls as it is preached or read – or as it is 'lifted off the page' by music in an oratorio or anthem or solo. For others worship may come alive when it is informal, with guitars to accompany the singing and many sharing. It is the Lord who makes it 'real.'

Corporate worship gives us special opportunities to be 'occupied with God' and great Sundays overflow into great Mondays to Saturdays in personal worship. Our daily times with God can be inspired and refreshed by Sunday's worship – in spirit, mind and body. There will be joy, praise, adoration – but, supremely, reverent submission.

'Let us be grateful for receiving a kingdom that cannot be shaken, and thus let us offer to God acceptable worship, with reverence and awe; for our God is a consuming fire.' (Hebrews 12.28-29)

8 APPROACH TO GOD

– With Penitence

We are (Hebrews 10.22) to 'draw near with a true heart in full assurance of faith', but 'with our hearts sprinkled clean from an evil conscience and our bodies washed with pure water.' As often as we come into the presence of God we come as sinners cleansed and forgiven through the blood of Christ. The worshipper must never forget the means of his being welcomed by God, must never approach God in an attitude of self-confidence. Our confidence is through Christ as Saviour and Mediator.

The Holy Communion Service supremely expresses, time and time again, for us and to God, that our salvation rests on the sacrifice made once for all upon the Cross. Whatever the season of the Church's year we celebrate it in the broken body and poured-out blood of Christ. Here is our spiritual birthright for eternity. Here is our assurance and confidence.

However, there is a distinction between that once-for-all sacrifice for sins and the need to go on being forgiven. You remember how Jesus spelt this out to Peter in the Upper Room (John 13). Peter had refused to have his feet washed by Jesus, but Jesus insisted. He distingished between the bath and the foot-washing – in our terms the bath and the hand-washing. Peter's preliminary resistance to any washing by Jesus then gave way to a request to be washed all over, but Jesus told him he had already been bathed and did not need to be bathed again. Modern-day Peters keep wanting some fresh assurance of forgiveness or acceptance by God and will frequently seek to be 're-converted' or 're-blessed' at a service or rally instead of grasping the fact of the 'bath' once and for all. However, on the other side of the coin are those who have grasped the truth of the 'bath' – they know Christ has forgiven them – but give scant attention to the foot-washing. This practical action was necessary several times a day, just as hand-washing is with us. The need for continuing spiritual cleansing and forgiveness is also necessary every day – even several times a day. Are we careless about this spiritual hygiene?

The words of I John 1.8-9 are addressed to Christians: 'If we say we have no sin, we deceive ourselves, and the truth is not in us. If we confess our sins, he is faithful and just, and will forgive our sins and cleanse us from all unrighteousness.' Such forgiveness is possible because of the Cross and because (2.1) we have an advocate with the Father, Jesus Christ the righteous.

In the foot-washing incident and in his emphasis on the words in the Lord's Prayer, 'Forgive us our sins . . .' Jesus meant us to take this seriously. It is a truth which dawns slowly on us that the more we go on in the Christian life the more we see sin and so the more we have to confess. Like Isaiah (Isaiah 6) the more we see God's holiness and majesty, the more we see ourselves in his light. Our self-interest, self-opinion, self-centredness and self-sufficiency become uncomfortably exposed. The shallowness of our love for God and of our love for our neighbour is thrown into contrast by the light of his marvellous love for us. We increasingly see sin not just as a regrettable weakness or failure but as an offence against our Lord and God.

Sometimes it helps us to open up to one another, as in James 5.16: 'Confess your sins to one another, and pray for one another.' This is not done lightly. Normally it would need to be in the security of a close friendship or of a confidential pastoral or counselling relationship. I have heard many confessions – walking in the grounds of a conference centre, sitting in my study, sharing in a side pew of the church, out in the country – but always with the opportunity to minister the word, to talk and then to pray with and for the person concerned. Sometimes it has involved weeks or months of help. The minister needs to be able to turn to others for similar fellowship too, perhaps to a fellow-minister or to a good friend in the church fellowship.

I am thankful to be in a church that has confession as part of its normal liturgy. Some people do not like it – they object to telling God they are sinners each time they come to worship. But perhaps that tells us more about their spiritual blindness than it does about the liturgy! In the days before hymns the service went straight into the sentences, such as I John 1.8-9, or Psalm 51: 'The sacrifice acceptable to God is a broken spirit; a broken and contrite heart, O God, you will not despise,' or Luke 15: 'I will arise and go to my father and I will say to him, Father, I have sinned against heaven and before you; I am no longer worthy to be called your son.' Then it moved into the exhortation about worship, but emphasising that first we must admit and confess our sins. The confession, for everyone to join in, accurately puts first the sins of omission: 'We have failed to do what we ought to have done' before the sins of commission: 'We have done what we ought not to have done.' The setting is that of the seriousness of sin, the need for mercy and restoration.

When I go to church services where confession is either ignored or merely included in a sentence of the minister's prayer I feel a deep lack in the whole approach to God. It is not just my feeling. There *is* a deep lack. If forgiveness is not taken seriously in corporate worship then it is unlikely to be taken seriously in personal prayer. As we saw earlier, what happens on Sundays should inspire and guide the pattern of our approach to God in the week. There should, however, be time for reflection and self-examination before a service begins if we are to join sincerely in the general act of confession – a further stimulus to preparation beforehand. And when services do not include a penitential opening then we will need to incorporate our own act of penitence in the quiet of our hearts before the service begins.

In our personal devotional prayer we can give more time and attention to self-examination. This is not to be morbid introspection but a real desire to walk more worthily of our Lord, to repent of sin and to know the joy of his forgiveness. There are various books of devotion that can help us. Some people value Lancelot Andrewes' *Preces Privatae*. He certainly opens up a wide range of thinking about sin and forgiveness, but is rather lacking in joy. I find Baillie's *A*

Diary for Private Prayer immensely helpful because it seems to relate more to every day living. All of us should have books like this, but we may find it also helpful to prepare our own 'spiritual check up' book. For instance, it might include questions like these:

Can I listen to other Christian workers being praised and not be jealous?

Can I hear of the 'success' of some other church or Christian work and not try to explain it away?

Can I be constructively criticised and not resent the criticiser?

Can I accept that my talents and gifts may be less noticed than gifts in some other Christians, even if they are just as useful for God?

What do I honestly regard as 'getting on in life' – is it in terms of Christian maturity, or of possessions and success?

What is the overriding ambition of my life – to be 'someone', or to serve Christ faithfully?

How much have I brought God into my thinking, planning and doing this day?

Has my love of God's Word grown cold?

What is my giving really like? Have I overhauled my giving recently, testing it by the standard of a tenth and more?

Do I want to give the least or the most?

What is my intercession like? Is it time to sort it out – perhaps simply by getting a new loose-leaf book to organise my praying, so that I can support many people and different aspects of work for the Lord?

Am I really concerned about the poverty of so much of the world and the social needs of my town?

What is my life-style? Is it hardly distinguishable from a non-Christian's?

Or is it a simpler style?

How good a listener am I to preaching and to other people's opinions?

Do I care about people – in my home, in my place of work, in my neighbourhood?

Is my evangelism sensitive, treating the other person with

respect and care, or do I bludgeon with the Gospel?

Am I prepared to let other people do the mundane jobs of moving chairs, preparing meals and serving others while I converse?

How grateful am I for food – for its supply and its preparation?

Do I have a standard of comfort for my home and a standard of austerity for my church?

Has any action or attitude of mine disgraced Christ this day? Has my temper flared? Have I acted selfishly?

Are there those who are not part of the church because I am?

Am I prepared to stand up for Christ anywhere, or am I sometimes ashamed or reluctant to be known as a Christian?

Did I really worship God last Sunday – or just go through the form of the service?

Have people looked at me to see Christ and been disappointed?

How much does the love of God flow through me to others?

Am I loyal to the Body of Christ, or do I needlessly criticise Christian things to unbelievers?

Am I scrupulously honest in my tax returns and my expenses claims?

Can people rely completely on my words?

Is my mouth clean and are my relationships pure?

Am I quick to see the wrongs of others but slow to see them in myself?

Do I make allowances for my own failings but not for the failings of others?

Am I a peace-maker? Am I quick to say 'sorry'?

Am I 'on track' with God's purposes for my life? If so, how far has that purpose been forwarded this month?

Lord, how do *you* see my life?' 'Create in me a clean heart, O God, and put a new and right spirit within me.'

We would do well to get the 'habit of penitence' into our daily lives as much as the habit of washing our hands. In the office we 'blow our top' over something. There'll need to be an apology to the people we have hurt. But what about God? Should we not pause, be open with the Lord and ask for his forgiveness there and then? We are reading a book or watching a film. Something really 'strikes home' in it, showing us a fault in ourselves that we had readily overlooked or ignored. It is a moment for reflection and then for confession and forgiveness. God speaks to us in so many ways and the Holy Spirit may at any time convict us of selfishness or lack of love or anything that is not in keeping with Christian living. Act on it, confess it, get cleansed.

Penitence is met by our Lord with mercy and grace. It is a wonderful fact that our Lord has shared human life and knows the problems of temptation. As Hebrews 4.15 says: 'He is not a high priest who is unable to sympathise with our weaknesses.' It is right that confession and forgiveness should be followed by praise and thanksgiving – with all the joy of those freshly cleansed, to worship and serve him. There is a rhythm to the Christian life, in this pattern. Where sin is not taken seriously the Christian misses the liberating joy and blessing of sins confessed, sins forgiven, and has a more monochrome Christian existence. He misses the depth of heartfelt praise expressed in so many hymns, for it is the person who is forgiven much who loves much, the person who sees the depth of the mercy of God who is constantly inspired in praise:

'Praise, my soul, the king of heaven;
To his feet thy tribute bring.
Ransomed, healed, restored, forgiven,
Who like me his praise should sing?'

9   APPROACH TO GOD
–With Praise and Thanksgiving(1)

Praise is to be a constant dimension in our Christian lives. 'Through him (Jesus) let us continually offer up a sacrifice of praise to God, that is, the fruit of lips that acknowledge his name.' (Hebrews 13.15). This text immediately reminds us that true praise is *to* God, *through* Jesus, and is a *fruit* of our submission to him as Lord and Saviour. So praise is *not* hymns, anthems, solos, psalms, oratorios or choruses. They are only the vehicles of praise. To join in hymns without a heart redeemed by the blood of Christ and renewed by the Holy Spirit is merely to sing words – it is not praise to the living God. The true desire and ability to 'sing a new song to the Lord' depends not on a music qualification but on a heart qualification, though it is a bonus if there is musical excellence as well! The bursts of praise in Scripture are always heart-bursts, in exclamation, in poetry and song.

What does it mean '*continually* to offer up a sacrifice of praise'? It will spring from an atmosphere of praise. My wife, Myrtle, comes from a family with many aunts and uncles. The oldest uncle particularly breathed a spirit of loving encouragement. Whenever you visited him he took a close interest in how things were going for you and that interest continued even when you could not visit. At the end of his life he went into a nursing home. We went to see him. He was full of admiration for the way the home was run, the kindness of all the nursing staff, the skill and care of the doctors, the help he received from everyone. 'They are all wonderful,' he said. Then we met some of the staff. 'What a wonderful man he is,' they said, 'so cheerful and kind – we love having him here.' That summed it all up. His spirit of kindness and encouragement overflowed – it was continual. When there was opportunity to express gratitude he did so naturally, not as a forced politeness.

So it is in the Christian life. We need to pray for an increasing spirit of praise and thanksgiving in our character and personality. Then when there are specific opportunities to join in times of corporate praise or to express personal thanksgiving it will be a natural focussing of what is already in our heart and not a forced exercise. You see this with Jesus. As he takes the food to distribute to the five thousand he gives thanks – naturally. When after the mission of the seventy the disciples return full of what has happened, 'in that same hour he rejoiced in the Holy Spirit and said "I thank you, Father, Lord of heaven and earth, that you have hidden these things from the wise and understanding and revealed them to babes."'

You see this in the beginning of the Church. In Luke 24.53 we are told that the disciples returned to Jerusalem with great joy and were continually in the temple praising God. In Acts 2.46: 'Day by day, attending the temple together and breaking bread in their homes, they partook of food with glad and generous hearts, praising God and having favour with all the people.' A spirit of praise indeed! But then read what follows: 'And the Lord added to their number day by day those who were being saved.' It looks as if the spirit of praise was a powerful witnessing force for evangelism. The 'popular' view of Christianity is that it takes away the joy of living and that Christians face a life of legalism and misery. What a lie! So when non-Christians see Christians around them who clearly have a spirit of praise it can have quite an impact. We often find that when non-Christians come into our church, with a large number of people genuinely worshipping and praising God from the heart, they are so impressed by it that they begin to seek Christ. Not that we need to keep shouting 'Hallelujah!' all the time or grinning. Life has much that is serious and sad, but the spirit of praise goes deep and you can sense it quietly there even in the times of weeping and sorrow.

Naturally, praise will spring to our lips when we hear of something special God has done, or a blessing in a person's life, or an answer to prayer. When we were facing the re-building of All Souls we found ourselves in a collision between the needs of a building to serve the Gospel and the interests of those wishing to preserve historic buildings. My colleague John Stott had earlier expressed this to a small meeting in Perth, Western Australia, and had said it looked as if a bomb on the church would be the simplest solution! A reporter circulated the story. It got conspicuous coverage in the British Press. Some years later, before the rebuilding commenced, there was a ring on the door-bell of the Rectory. Two police officers were standing there. I invited them into the entrance hall. 'We have to inform you, sir, that we have received a telephone call saying that a bomb has been planted in your church.' Before I knew what I was saying, I responded: 'Praise the Lord!' The police officers were somewhat taken aback! The telephone call proved to be a hoax, but it was a memorable moment!

The bigger test of the spirit of praise is when we are facing the difficulties of life. The example of Paul and Silas beaten with rods, put into the inner prison, their feet in the stocks, praying and singing hymns to God at midnight is an outstanding triumph of praise. It is an example that thousands of other prisoners for the Lord have been enabled to follow down through Christian history and in the present day. Paul later wrote (I Thessalonians 5.16): 'Rejoice always, pray constantly, give thanks in all circumstances; for this is the will of God in Christ Jesus for you.'

It is important to get this clear: '*in* all circumstances', not '*for* all circumstances.' The idea of praising God for disasters, tragedies and illnesses has gained currency amongst some Christians in recent years. It is put across as the way of high Christian living, of triumphant faith. But is it really a Biblical view?

One night the telephone rang. I listened as the person, telephoning from far away, explained that his son was in great trouble – his marriage had broken up, he had no job, he had nowhere to live, he was an alcoholic. Then it happened. He went on: 'Of course, we are praising God that his marriage has broken up, he has no job, nowhere to live and that he's an alcoholic.' My blood ran cold. Praising God for those things? That seemed more like 'positive thinking' than a cause for Christian praise.

If, however, we are going to praise God *in* those circumstances rather than *for* them, then we are on a strong Biblical footing. Look at I Thessalonians 5.16. This is certainly the triumph of praise: that nothing can separate us from the love of God, that there is a way back to God for that man in his marriage break-up and alcoholism. Yes! It is Christian to praise God in the midst of bereavement – praising for his presence and comfort, praising for his assurance of eternal life. It is Christian to praise God in illness – praising him that he has power to heal or bring other blessings out of this experience. It is Christian to praise God in disasters – praising that he is with us in this experience and can bring his purposes to fruition through it all. But that is all different from praising *for* all circumstances.

But what about Ephesians 5.20, some will say? 'Always and for everything giving thanks in the name of our lord Jesus Christ to God the Father'. This is certainly the spirit of praise – the verse is preceded with an exhortation to praise in music. But can this text's 'for everything' actually mean that I should thank God for someone living immorally, or for my friend being killed in a road accident, or for a person going blind, or someone being cruel to his wife. If so, I am being asked to praise for evil and nowhere in the Scriptures is such a thing countenanced. The very opposite is true and the rest of this chapter of Ephesians spells it out: 'Immorality and all impurity must not be named among you ... because of these things the wrath of God comes upon the sons of disobedience ... walk as children of the light (for the fruit of the light is found in all that is good and right and true) ... take no part in the unfruitful works of darkness, but instead *expose* them'. Evil is to be avoided or fought or exposed. Death is 'an enemy.' (I Corinthians 15.26) When the devil is cast finally into the lake of fire we shall not say: 'Praise the Lord for the devil', but 'Praise the Lord – evil has gone for ever.'

The idea behind praising for cruelty and wrong, some say, is that it shows we trust God as in control. But that trust is basic to Christian conviction in any case. We *do* believe he is Lord and that 'in everything God works for

57

good with those who love him, who are called according to his purpose.' We testify to the way in which he has brought good out of evil, blessing out of disaster, and healing out of sickness. We do not have to praise for evil to demonstrate this conviction. Jesus never does. Nor do any of the Apostles.

The key to triumph is in being able to separate the problem or circumstance from our spirit of praise. Let me explain. When the seventy return from their mission in Luke 10, they are full of praise for what has happened. Jesus says to them: 'Do not rejoice in this, that the spirits are subject to you, but rejoice that your names are written in heaven.' The fount of praise is constant – it is in our salvation and our belonging to the Lord. If it is in circumstances then it will go 'high' or 'low' according to what is happening to us. Like a car without the clutch depressed, the engine and gears are so linked that the engine will stall during slow running. The clutch brings release and allows the engine to run even when the car is waiting at the traffic lights. We have to learn to 'depress the clutch' in our Christian lives and then in *all* circumstances we can find cause for praise – 'continually' offering the sacrifice of praise. To put it simply, I do not say, 'Everything's awful. I can't praise,' nor 'Everything's awful, praise the Lord!' nor 'Everything's awful, praise the Lord for the awfulness,' but 'Everything's awful, but I praise the Lord that he is the Lord and he is with me in this experience and will bring me through.'

When my wife and I were in the USA at a conference last year, I was speaking on this theme. Afterwards a couple came up to me. 'We can't wait to telephone our daughter. She has been diagnosed a diabetic and we have constantly told her that she will not get the victory until she praises God for her diabetes. And she has replied each time, "I can't." Now we are going to tell her she needn't do so, but can have victory through praising God *in* her diabetic state.' I hope that girl has found the power of praising God *in* all circumstances.

So let us pray for the Holy Spirit to deepen the fount of praise and thanksgiving in our lives, that it may be a continual witness to the Lord's grace. Then when opportunity arises to praise him specially, lifting our hearts to him several times during the day, or as we come together with other Christians or as we kneel alone to meet with him, let us praise out of the depths of thankful hearts. Sometimes that will be in the quietness of awe and adoration. It may be in tears as in Ezra 3 at the foundation of the temple rebuilding when the older people wept with joy while the younger ones shouted. It may be with great music, with organ and orchestras. It may be informally with guitars, choruses and spiritual songs. It may be in spontaneous phrases of praise. It may be in giving for the Lord's work – money and time. It may be in renewed lives of commitment. We may use hymns, psalms, poems, songs, recorded music, devotional books of praise. We may compile our own anthologies of praise. But let us, through Christ, continually offer up a sacrifice of praise to God, that is, the fruit of lips that acknowledge his name. Keep praising!

10 APPROACH TO GOD

– With Praise and Thanksgiving(2)

If our praise and thanksgiving is not to get into a rut, it needs constant refreshing and extension of its range of content. So it is right to ask next: for what do we praise? I found my praising widened in scope and enriched in depth when I worked through the Scriptures and found six main themes of praise:

1 FOR GOD HIMSELF

We are to praise God as God – revelling in the wonder of who he is and all that he means to us. Such praise abounds in the heart of the psalmist: 'I call upon the Lord, who is worthy to be praised' (Psalm 18.3);
'Who is God, but the Lord? And who is a rock, except our God?' (Psalm 18.31);
'O Lord, our Lord, how majestic is your name in all the earth!' (Psalm 8.1);
'The Lord reigns; he is robed in majesty; the Lord is robed, he is girded with strength ... Your throne is established from of old; you are from everlasting' (Psalm 93);
'O come, let us sing to the Lord, ... for the Lord is a great God ... he is our God.' (Psalm 95);
'O sing to the Lord a new song; sing to the Lord, all the earth' (Psalm 96);
'Great is the Lord and greatly to be praised ... ascribe to the Lord the glory due to his name' (Psalm 96).

It is a bubbling over of adoration. It is the joy of the child in his wonderful Father. It is the glorying in the fact that he who has made us his for ever is God – none greater, none more powerful – and with no human limitations or fallibility. He will fulfil his word and one day will gather his vast redeemed family with him in the new heavens and the new earth. As we live in a world where we wonder what is going to happen next, where world events move with breathless rapidity, where political powers exercise their sway often with terrible effects, we can stand back, look up and get things back into perspective. Whatever man does, nothing can separate us from God. He is King. He is Lord. He is in control.

So often I will just revel in God. And when I have the opportunity to do so in a large crowd of believing people, singing his praise with all my heart, that is marvellous. 'King of kings and Lord of lords – Alleluia!' But often it will be alone, walking down the street, meditating on his word, or waking up to a new day. He is God, and worthy to be praised. And as I see in some new way his character – his steadfast love, his faithfulness, his patience, his mercy, his kindness, his righteousness, his power – I am again stimulated to praise him. The more we know him, the more we will want to praise him.

2 CREATION

The psalmist lived nearer to the evidences of God's creation than those of us who live in cities. He had an eye for the touch of the Lord:
Psalm 19: 'The heavens are telling the glory of God; and the firmament proclaims his handiwork'.
Psalm 24: 'The earth is the Lord's and the fulness thereof'.
In Psalm 29 he observes the storm in the forest: 'The voice of the Lord is upon the waters; the voice of the Lord breaks the cedars; the voice of the Lord makes the oaks to whirl, and strips the forests bare; and in his temple all cry "Glory!"'
Or the great Psalm 104, so full of loving appreciation for the majesty of God's creation: 'O Lord, how manifold are your works! In wisdom you have made them all; the earth is full of your creatures.'
The song of the seraphim in Isaiah 6 is that of creation: 'Holy, holy, holy is the Lord of hosts; the whole earth is full of his glory.' It is the song that we shall share as part of the

heavenly praise (Revelation 4.11): 'Worthy are you, our Lord and God, to receive glory and honour and power, for you created all things, and by your will they existed and were created.'

Even if you have grown up with an appreciation of beauty in creation, when you came to a living faith in Christ you see it all in new depth and with fresh meaning. As the hymn puts it, earth beneath becomes 'sweeter green' and sky above 'softer blue.' This happens because instead of just admiring the beauty you begin to praise the Creator of the beauty. Standing on a mountain top, gazing across the gigantic peaks around you, or seeing the wonder of growth in a seedling bravely flourishing in a windowbox, your heart praises the Creator.

It is a surprise to find that not everyone appreciates the beauty around – not even all Christians. Coming out of the city of Manchester years ago, we headed for the Peak district with a party of city lads. We climbed to the top of Mam Tor and gazed across the marvellous panorama of hills and valleys. In the far distance there was a cement factory and a chimney belching smoke. 'Ah, reality!' said one of the lads.

We took another group for a holiday in some of the lovelier parts of Southern England. Time and again we would pause while driving along and say: 'Look at that!' The view thrilled my wife and myself – but not our passengers. 'Oh, yes!' they replied and then went on with their conversation. Part of Christian responsibility is to open people up to the wonders of creation – to the good, lovely and beautiful things around us. It is good that Christians develop hobbies and interests like watching birds, mountain-climbing, walking, and holidaying in places of scenic grandeur. It is good that they develop an interest in the arts, in music, design and artistic appreci-ation. There is so much which is sordid around us, thanks to sinful man, that we need to make an effort to enjoy the lovely things of the world. For city dwellers this will mean more frequent trips out of the city so as to keep a balance in life.

Increasingly, the joy of creation will turn to praise – the

first buds of spring on the trees, the first new flowers after the winter, the kaleidoscope of colours in the trees of autumn, the magnificence of a sunset, the delicacy of frost on the trees, the scenery of mountains, lakes and forests, the variety of animals, the miracle of birth and growth, the resources of the earth, the abilities to create and invent, life itself in all its fulness. Think of the Creator and there is an endless arena of praise!

We will want to make this a deliberate part of our regular pattern of praise and thanksgiving as well as the spontaneous praise of the moment of seeing. Think back over each day to what you have seen of God's manifold creation – in the big and the small – and give him thanksgiving.

In the beautiful town of Olney, Buckinghamshire, John Newton and William Cowper wrote hymns and poems that go on inspiring us centuries later. The town is set beside the River Ouse, with the old cottages and the great church with its tall spire surrounded by meadows, trees and flowers. In this setting, William Cowper wrote, in 'The Task':

> 'Happy who walks with him! Whom what he finds
> Of flavour or of scent in fruit or flow'r
> Or what he views of beautiful or grand
> In nature, from the broad, majestic oak
> To the green blade that twinkles in the sun,
> Prompts with remembrance of a present God!'

3 THE WORD

Praise for God's revelation of himself through creation is matched in Psalm 19 by praise for God's revealing of his laws and ways – 'The law of the Lord is perfect, reviving the soul . . . the precepts of the Lord are right, rejoicing the heart.' Psalm 119 is an anthem of praise for all that God's Word can mean to our lives. The Word directs our praise. 'I will praise you with an upright heart, when I learn your righteous ordinances' (v.7). It enriches us: 'In the way of your testimonies I delight as much as in all riches' (v.14). it is a constant source of praise: 'At midnight I rise to praise you, because of your righteous ordinances' (v.62) . . . 'Seven times a day . . . ' (v.164).

Of course, the Psalmist is not praising for the Word itself but for the way it brings him hope, assurance, comfort, guidance, strength and understanding. By obeying the Word he proves God's faithfulness, steadfast love and righteousness. The Word is to him better than riches and sweeter than honey. He loves the law – the Word – and meditates upon it.

We are hardly likely to want to praise God for his Word unless we have really come to it in love and obedience. An arm's length relationship with the Scriptures, a polite respect for them, a listening without submission to their truth, a selective use of them as it suits us or a manipulating of them to support our theories, will not produce praise.

It is when the Word becomes the living Word to us that we begin to praise. I was in my twenties before I turned to the Lord in sincerity and commitment. My Christianity before that had not been insincere, not without study of the Bible, but now it became 'for real.' This was the promised re-birth of the Holy Spirit opening me up to God, but at the same time opening me to his Word. I suddenly began to 'hunger for the Word,' sitting up into the night to read it.

Imagine this world without the Word of God brought to us 'in many and various ways and in these last days spoken to us by a Son' – this Word which proves itself as God's Word when we trust it and seek to obey it – this Word which has given authority to the Christian message, and has been the means of millions of people coming into salvation, the guide and teacher of the truth and ways of our God, the comforter to so many. What other book could we turn to every day of our lives and find fresh inspiration as the Holy Spirit opens it up to us?

If we love the Word of God then let us praise him for it – praise him when he has shown us something new in our meditation on it, or when he has convicted us of sin or challenged us to action, or when he has revealed more of himself and his character to us, or when he has opened it up to someone else we have been counselling, or when he has brought it to our mind in a moment of need. Let us praise and thank the Lord for his Word and show our praise by being doers of the Word and not hearers only.

4 SALVATION

A never-ending source of praise is salvation. In the Old Testament it was the redemption from slavery which brought forth frequent praise. God had delivered his people in his steadfast love. For us, as New Testament believers, the redemption is of course in Christ, delivering us from the slavery of sin, reconciling God and man, opening the gate of eternal life. We worship Christ by that special title 'Saviour,' the title with which his birth was announced to the world. It is heart-rending that some Christians react from the word 'save.' Probably they do so because of some unfortunate misuse of the word or because they associate it with a particular form of evangelism. But if they do so they avoid one of the greatest words of the Christian faith. Even today, in our daily newspaper, the word 'save' still means a rescue, a snatching from destruction. We use it of people saved from a sinking ship or a car accident or a fire. Perhaps the word only means much to us when we realise from what we have been saved – the division between perishing and eternal life (John 3.16), destruction and life (Matthew 7.13-14) or condemnation and salvation. (John 3.17)

When John Newton wrote 'Amazing Grace' at Olney he wrote it as a man who had known the depths of sin before coming to Christ and thus from a full heart of praise wrote:

'Amazing grace! (how sweet the sound!)
That saved a wretch like me!
I once was lost, but now am found,
Was blind, but now I see.'

There was a time when I could not have echoed those words. One night the minister of the church where I was a youth said in the middle of his sermon: 'Stand up, all who know they are saved!' There was a furore after the service! 'How dare those people stand up! How presumptuous and precocious of them – none of us will know we are saved until the judgement day.' It was only slowly that I began to see how wrong this criticism was. Those who stood had come to acknowledge they could never be good enough for God and so, as sinners, had put their trust in Christ's sacrifice for their sins on the Cross. Far from being 'presumptuous' about their own worthiness they 'presumed' on Christ – exactly as God intended. When I saw this, I could begin to share John Newton's praise.

It will be one of the two greatest themes of praise in heaven. Alongside praise of God as Creator, we will sing to Jesus, the Lamb of God: 'Worthy are you . . . for you were slain and by your blood you ransomed men for God, from every tribe and tongue and people and nation, and have made them a kingdom and priests to our God.' (Revelation 5.9)

This praise bursts out in the New Testament. I Peter 1.3-9 is a hymn of praise for redemption - 'Blessed be the God and Father of our Lord Jesus Christ!' . . . for mercy, being born anew to a living hope, an inheritance in heaven, the salvation of our souls.

This praise bursts out in our services and liturgy. The great celebration of the Holy Communion is described as a 'sacrifice of praise and thanksgiving.' We come to a Christian funeral service with a high note of triumphant praise amidst the sadness of bereavement, because death has lost its sting in Christ's death and resurrection and we rejoice in the living hope of eternal life. Thousands of hymns and poems have been written glorying in our salvation. It is a constant theme of praise. Let it be so in our lives. Let us never tire individually and corporately of praising God for his salvation.

5 DEEDS

Specific praise and specific thanks follow God's specific interventions or answers to prayer or blessings in the life of the Biblical writers and Christians through the centuries.

'I waited patiently for the Lord; he inclined to me and heard my cry. He drew me out of the desolate pit.... set my feet upon a rock ... he put a new song in my mouth, a song of praise to our God.' Psalm 40.

In II Corinthians 1, Paul writes of the afflictions he has had to face, but praises God for the comfort received and the deliverance given. He goes on to urge the Corinthians to join in helping by prayer, so that many will be able to share in the thanksgiving when God answers.

We all tend to be like the boy visiting another person's house with his mother. They sit down to tea. In the centre of the table is a huge cream and chocolate cake. The boy is quietly told by his mother that he cannot start with the cake. He eats the snadwiches dutifully. At last, time for cake. The hostess cuts a piece and passes it to him. 'What do you say?' says his mother. 'Got it!' comes the reply. We are so like this with God. We pray about all sorts of things. We ask, we receive. How often do we give specific thanks?

As we end the day, we should deliberately cast our mind back through its events, particularly those for which we have prayed in the morning, and give thanks. Some people keep a special prayer diary alongside their normal pattern of prayer. In this they put the various requests – not least when other people ask for prayers. On the opposite page they record the answers. That turns to thanksgiving.

In our church gatherings for prayer we must start with praise and thanksgiving. The leader will keep notes from the previous meeting so that he can share the specific answers given, but others around the room will share their own specific thanksgivings. It is enormously encouraging to share in thanksgiving – for the way God has healed, for specific answers to prayer for an evangelistic service, for help in finding a job or somewhere to live, for particular experiences of God's upholding. Some people also have an extra-special time of thanksgiving on their birthday or the last day of the year or at some other significant point in their year. They look back and thank the Lord.

67

As the psalmist says (Psalm 107.1): 'Give thanks to the Lord, for he is good, for his steadfast love endures for ever.'

6 PEOPLE

One of the surprises to me in researching the themes of praise was that Paul frequently thanked God for his friends. In his letters to the Romans, I Corinthians, Ephesians, Philippians, Colossians, both Thessalonian letters, both letters to Timothy and Philemon, he gives thanks for some aspect of those to whom he is writing even when he is about to correct or criticise them. I find this challenging. I am much more ready to jump into criticism of someone without looking for aspects to praise about them! Paul is thankful for their faith, their service, their friendship, their partnership in the Gospel, their love, their salvation. The spirit of praise keeps coming to the surface in Paul's writing.

I found it a new dimension to praise for my friends. Of course I had done so before, but now I began to thank with more thought and a far wider coverage of people.

We need to let our minds range across our friends and colleagues, and our fellow churchmembers whom we meet but who are not close friends. We can gather into our thanksgiving leaders and helpers, observing and giving thanks for acts of kindness, thoughtfulness, generosity, encouragement, faithfulness. We need to learn to praise for good qualities and deeds even in people whom we find it difficult to get along with. Thank the Lord for those who were out visiting house-to-house this week, those who made the coffee for you to drink after morning service, those who care for the elderly and the children, those who cleaned the church and stacked the chairs, those who worked long hours preparing for preaching, those young people standing up for God and his truth against mocking and opposition at college . . . the list is endless. Look round and widen your thanksgiving and praise for people!

One of the richest expressions of thanksgiving is in 'The General Thanksgiving.' It would be good to use it frequently as a summary of our thanking and praising:

'Almighty God, Father of all mercies,
We your unworthy servants give you our humble and
heartfelt thanks
for all your goodness and loving kindness
to us and to all men.
We praise you for our creation, preservation,
and all the blessings of this life,
but above all for your amazing love in the redemption
of the world by our Lord Jesus Christ,
for the means of grace and for the hope of glory.
We pray that you will give us such an awareness
of your goodness
that our hearts may be truly thankful,
and that we may declare your praise
not only with our lips but in our lives,
by giving ourselves in your service
and by walking before you in holiness and righteousness all our days.
All honour and glory be to you,
Father, Son and Holy Spirit,
now and throughout eternity. Amen.'

11   APPROACH TO GOD

In a New Relationship
(1) As Children to the Father

The invitation to call God 'Father' was made by Jesus himself. We take it almost for granted, yet what a privilege it is! The title in all its richness deflects us from treating God with irreverent 'chumminess.' The Lord's Prayer follows the title 'Father' with 'hallowed be thy name' and directs us away from such a lack of reverence. Yet to be entitled, through Jesus, to call the living God 'Father' – , coming to him as his child, speaking to him with the openness of a child to a Father – is wonderful. Revel in this relationship and all it means!

The concept is spelt out for us by Jesus in Luke 11. There he teaches 'The Lord's Prayer' and goes on to show us three things about the Father's attitude to us as his children:

1 A LOVING RELATIONSHIP

As sons to a father (v.11), as children to a father (v.13), so are we to our God. The wider sense of the term 'children of God' referring to all humanity is not intended here. Indeed, the New Testament frequently emphasises that in Christ the father-son terminology is to be applied to the special relationship of God to the believer.

So John's prologue (John 1.12): 'But to all who received him, who believed in his name, he gave power to become children of God,' is crystal clear. So is Romans 8.15-17, speaking of life in the Spirit after being justified by faith: 'You received the Spirit of sonship. When we cry 'Abba! Father! it is the Spirit himself bearing witness with our spirit that we are children of God.' So is the deep glorying of I John 3.1: 'See what love the Father has given us, that we should be called children of God; and so we are.' When we believed in Christ we were made part of the Father's family – adopted, his for ever. I hope you are sure of this in your own life and that the joy of it frequently overwhelms you – perhaps in the depth of real Christian fellowship, benefitting from brothers and sisters in Christ whose love is genuine and practical, perhaps in the peaks of worship as part of his family or perhaps in moments when he seems to touch you with some special token of his love.

In an earthly family we usually share a lot of time together – eating together, holidaying together, discussing together and planning together. My daughter and sons have always been able to slip into my study to tell me their bicycle chain has fallen off or to ask a question, or to sit in the kitchen chatting things over with their mother. We do not always find it convenient, but it is part of family life.

Our God wants us to have a similar relationship with him. He is our 'heavenly Father' and that word 'heavenly' does not mean 'remote,' but rather that he is not restricted like an earthly father – he is always ready to hear and his answers are always perfect.

It was at theological college that I first began to 'see' this relationship. Some of my fellow students were clearly on much more open terms with God than I had known. Although worship and prayer meant a lot to me, I tended to keep them in their special slots. These fellows would pray about a letter or an essay or a problem and would expect the Lord to answer. And he seemed to do so! They talked to God about all sorts of things and at any time of the day. They simply 'slipped into his study' as sons to a Father.

I still have much to learn about developing this relationship. I'm more likely to pray at points during the day when I am meeting a crisis or when there is some special joy or encouragement, than I am in the more normal course of events. I need to make a conscious resolve to share things with my Father – facing an interview, making a journey, looking for a place to park, coping with limited finances, getting things done when there seems too much to do in a short time, remembering a friend who is having an operation or taking an exam, turning world news into prayer.

Such a relationship opens me also to my Father's

correction and discipline – 'The Lord disciplines him whom he loves.' (Hebrews 12.6) I can hardly bring things to him in prayer if I am consciously doing things which are against his truth and standards or in defiance of his guidance.

It is the privilege of all this which overwhelms me constantly. This infinitesimal piece of humanity is invited and encouraged to come at any time to the God who made the whole universe, the 'I am' of eternity, and call him 'Father.' It's simply marvellous.

2 A LOVING READINESS

Jesus must have been a vivid storyteller. He used such everyday illustrations that his hearers identified with them readily and so remembered what he said. The story he tells us in Luke 11.5 onwards has always been one that has come alive for me – the knocking up of a friend at midnight to ask for bread. Poor chap – fast asleep and snug, suddenly waking up and trying to think straight. We all know the feeling! Parents know it when the baby cries in the night: 'Whose turn is it?' and one has to drag out of bed while the other turns over and goes back to sleep! It is a hazard of the ministry to get woken up occasionally in the night (but not as often as doctors are). One night when we were in Manchester the doorbell rang and rang. It was about 3am. I eventually woke up and realised it was the doorbell. Then to stagger out of bed, find slippers and dressing gown, put on lights, get the front door keys and make one's way down the staircase of the big old Rectory to the front door. A man was standing there. I noticed that the floodlights were still on, lighting up the church alongside the Rectory – we had obviously forgotten to turn them off when going to bed. I opened the door. The man said: 'Is your spire really as tall as it looks?'

So I have sympathy with the man in Jesus' story! He was an earthly father and it needed a considerable amount of persuasive cajoling to get him out of bed to help. Strangely, some people take this as a picture of persistent prayer – of going on praying until God answers – but, of course, it is actually the drawing of a contrast between the earthly father and the heavenly Father. With the heavenly Father it is, 'Ask, and it will be given you; seek, and you will find; knock, and it will be opened to you.' Our God is always 'at the ready.' As the hymn puts it:

> 'There is an eye that never sleeps
> Beneath the wing of night;
> There is an ear that never shuts,
> When sink the beams of light.'

So I can turn to him in prayer at any time and in any place – in a bus, on a train, walking down the street, working in the kitchen, lying in bed, sitting at my desk, changing a car wheel or queuing in the supermarket.

3 A LOVING RICHNESS

Luke 11 encourages us further. The way in which an earthly father responds to requests is not likely to be perverse – giving a serpent instead of a fish, or a scorpion instead of an egg. We usually take much care in selecting gifts for birthdays and Christmas for those we love. We trudge round the shops with our lists and compare the varieties available, trying to get the best we can and the one most suitable to a particular person. The amateur photographer wants some special new lens, the mechanically – minded four-year-old wants something with which he can make things, the older friend just retiring from work wants a really comfortable garden chair, the teenager wants a watch like 'everybody else has' and so on down the list. Love takes care to respond.

Now we have already seen that the foundations of prayer do not let us treat God like a 'Father Christmas,' there to dole out what our selfishness wants. However, we can trust him to give the best gifts. As Jesus says, even sinful human fathers do quite well in choosing good gifts. How much more our heavenly Father who is perfect and untainted by sin. His gifts and blessings come through the gracious agency of the Holy Spirit. The parallel passage in Matthew 7.11 says: 'How much more will your Father who is in heaven give good things to those who ask him.' The whole context is of gifts in answer to prayer (not, of course, of a first-time receiving of the Holy Spirit). So the readiness of our Father to answer prayer is matched by his discernment and loving wisdom. He wants the best for us as his children and that best will be in terms of his will and purposes, not in feeding our selfish desires. He responds to us out of love.

As we bring our requests to him we need to be conscious of our fallibility, our limited vision and our sinfulness. Trust him to know how best to answer. S.D. Gordon wrote: 'If God were to say to me, "I want to give you a special love-gift – what would you like?" I would say, "Dear God, *you* choose." He knows what I would most enjoy and he would choose something finer than I would think.' That deliberate trust on our side is an expression of our submission as his children and our thankfulness that we can come and place ourselves and our needs into the wonderful love and security of a heavenly Father.

12   APPROACH TO GOD

In a New Relationship
(2) *As Bride to the Bridegroom*

As we go on in the Christian life we discover a deepening closeness to our Lord as expressed in John 15: 'As the Father has loved me, so have I loved you, abide in my love.' 'Abide in me and I in you.' It is the language of intimacy, of union, of love.

Love needs time. She sat down in the row in front of mine just as the lecture began. Her flaxen hair bounced as she laughed. There was something special about her. A few months later I went on a mission in Leeds and the same girl was part of the team on the mission. Two actresses were attracted to Christ during that mission, but did not come to faith. They worked in London and so 'the girl' and I were asked to follow them up. We took them to a Crusade meeting and they came to Christ. But another 'follow-up' was developing! I could not believe that this attractive girl could be interested in me. My college friends teased me. At last, I plucked up courage and invited her to tea. She said 'yes.' She responded again when I asked her out. We walked in the Kentish countryside and prayed in the village church at Ide Hill. We spent more and more time together. Eventually I 'popped the question' – on the unromantic railway platform of Penge West Station! Then we spent more time together. The wedding took place. Since then we have spent more time together!

Love needs time. Even if it is 'love at first sight,' the enrichment of love is never instant. If I had said to Myrtle: 'I can spare you five minutes on Monday, I'm too busy on Tuesday, perhaps ten minutes or so on Wednesday if I'm not too tired, I might squeeze in fifteen minutes on Thursday, though Friday is unlikely, Saturday should be all right for an hour or two, depending on what's on the Television, and a couple of hours on Sunday (sorry if I arrive late),' there would not have been much enrichment of love. Love in courtship or marriage, and love in friendship, needs spending time together, getting to know one another.

So it is in our love relationship with Jesus. It may begin with 'love at first sight' or be the result of a gradual approach to love, but enrichment of that love needs a lifetime – and beyond! When a girl is in love she is excited. 'I'll be seeing Peter today!' There is anticipation. The time is not begrudged. Is that how we love the Lord? Is time spent with him a burden, a nuisance, something to be fitted in? Or is it anticipated with delight? If our daily times of devotion and prayer have become dry or difficult or mere discipline, might it be that we have stopped seeing those times as with *him*?

The Bible speaks of Jesus as the bridegroom and we, his Church, as the bride. The newly-married need to learn to 'give and take.' There is much to learn about one another. A friend of mine did everything possible to avoid the hotel knowing that he and his wife were on their honeymoon, but when the porter said: 'Would you like morning tea, sir?' he turned to his wife and said: 'Do you like ... ' The words froze on his lips! We learn to adjust to one another – what sort of supper drink, holidays of scenery or beach, mustard with ham, cloves in apple pie, the use of money, standards of hospitality, what brings joy or pain.

But it is completely different in our relationship with Jesus. He is perfect. He does not need to adjust to us. Indeed, he also knows us through and through. 'As Christ loved the church and gave himself up for her (us), that he might sanctify her (us), having cleansed her (us) by the washing of water with the word, that he might present the church to himself in splendour, without spot or wrinkle or any such thing, that she (we) might be holy and without blemish.' (Ephesians 5.25) Christ wants us to press on towards perfection. He wants us to be lovelier and lovelier as people – growing in his grace and the fruit of the Spirit. The adaptation is entirely on our side. We are to adapt to Christ.

He meets our love with his: 'If a man loves me, he will

keep my word, and my Father will love him, and we will come to him and make our home with him.' (John 14.23). There are times when that love overwhelms us, when it is a 'mountain top' experience, or when we want to cry with wonder as we are touched by his loving action, kindness or thoughtfulness. Christianity is a love affair. We will want to respond to that love. At times we will want to break our 'alabaster box' of sacrificial devotion, or to respond in praise and worship, or in going, serving, caring, daring for him.

Such love needs time – time alone, time apart. It is vital to every Christian and especially to those who lead or minister. As Spurgeon said to ministers: 'If you become lax in sacred devotion not only will you need to be pitied but your people also, and the day cometh in which you will need to be ashamed and confounded.' The danger of the Christian minister is to 'be too busy to pray' whereas he needs to pray more. William Wilberforce wrote: 'I must secure more time for private devotions. I have been living far too public for me. The shortening of the devotions starves the soul; it grows lean and faint'.

The fundamental question is: 'Do we *want* to change? Do we *want* to grow more like Christ?' For a few months during the Second World War, I was evacuated from London to a village in Leicestershire. I was a choirboy at home, so joined the choir of that village's church. The choirmaster decided that the voices of another evacuee and I could benefit from some extra choral training. He was persuasive and told us to come to his house on the Wednesday evening at 7pm. That was also the last night that a film about a haunted house was being shown at the local cinema. We wanted to see it. We went to the choirmaster's house with dragging feet. Hope rose when we found he had not come back from a meeting. We waited, looking at the clock. He still did not come. We took courage in both hands and spoke to his wife: 'He will be tired when he gets in – he will need to eat – he won't feel like training voices . . . ' She let us go. We ran as fast as we could. At a road junction we spied the choirmaster pacing towards us in the darkness. We ran faster, in the other direction. We saw the film. It wasn't worth the effort!

The key to that incident was that we did not particularly *want* to have our voices improved. It is the key to our spending time in personal devotion, too. Do I want the Master Gardener to prune this branch of the vine? Do I want to be strengthened with might by his Spirit? Do I want to know more of his love? Do I want to be filled with all the fullness of God? Do I want to be more holy, more worthy of the Bridegroom? If so, I will ensure that I have time apart with my Lord, day by day and at other special times.

First, let's be practical about 'day by day.' Jesus said, 'When you pray, go into your room and shut the door and pray to your Father who is in secret?' (Matthew 6.6) The primary reason for his saying this was to avoid 'praying for show.' However, the principle of being alone is good to aim at. If we have a room of our own there is no problem, but not everyone has such a privilege. Is there anywhere to get apart? Perhaps by going to a local park? If not, can we shut out distractions of noise, putting hands over our ears? Kneeling is a helpful posture for many. Certainly Jesus knelt (Luke 22.41); there are numerous references to kneeling in the Acts of the Apostles; Paul says: 'I bow my knees' in Ephesians 3.14. But kneeling may be unhelpful. Posture of the body needs to allow our spirit to commune with the Lord. That may mean keeping the body moving, walking up and down the room, if sleepiness threatens. And what about atmosphere? Are you affected by your surroundings? At college some men did nothing to their rooms – they were basic and 'cold.' It did not worry them at all. Others of us made our rooms 'friendly' with furnishing and pictures. It mattered to us. If possible, I like to pray in 'friendly' surroundings or in the beauty of the Lord's creation. The growth of love-relationship with the Lord is helped for me in lovely surroundings – but it *can* be as real in the midst of the sordidness and clamour of the inner city.

When should daily devotion take place? A card beside a desk in our church office says, 'Is there life before breakfast?' If the morning is impossible for any length of personal devotion, at least greet the Lord! Sometimes when we say we cannot get up to pray we deceive ourselves. Thousands of people get up in time to jog, to decorate their faces, to eat – so why not to pray? Nevertheless, for many it is better to be apart with the Lord later in the day – in the lunchtime (using a church near our work?), or getting home from work, at the end of the day. If you love him and want to love him more, you will not have to 'find' time or 'make' time – it will be a priority in your day, and priorities get first claim on time.

Secondly, let's be practical about the special times of being apart. We do not know whether Jesus went apart every day. We assume so, as he walked closely with his Father. However, we *do* know that he had some special times apart, particularly after times of pressure, as the crowds pressed upon him in Mark 1 and Mark 3. When choosing the twelve he spent the whole night in prayer (Luke 6). After the mission of the disciples and John's beheading (Mark 6) he went apart; before turning towards Jerusalem he went up to the Mount of Transfiguration; before the Cross he went apart in Gethsemane. If Jesus needed to do this, how much more do we need to get apart – occasionally or regularly. We may call it a 'retreat' or 'getting away.' Some make it at least an annual event, as a time of re-evaluation. Alan Stibbs, the beloved expositor and lecturer, used to speak of the 'one decisive Lent' of his life when he sorted out God's way forward for him. Like Jesus, we may need to match these special times away to times of pressure or of new challenges.

The benefit of these times away is that we can relax and unwind. The telephone, the urgent requests, the decision-making, the non-stop whirl of activity – all are left behind. The dust settles and we begin to experience the 'restoration of the soul' spoken of in Psalm 23 – the atmosphere of the 'still waters' and 'green pastures.' It can be enormously helpful to have such times in beautiful surroundings. Some of the most glorious times of restoration for me have been in the mountains of Switzerland. After a time of particular pressure some Christian friends paid for my wife and I to have a short 'luxury' holiday. We went first class on the train to Cornwall and over on the helicopter to the Scilly Isles. The next four days were spent in the beauty of the islands, going out in boats morning and afternoon, staying at a lovely hotel overlooking the sea. Our souls were restored. Of course, these are very special experiences. There are nearer places of beauty and, for some, enjoying beauty in music and art is restorative. Not that this beauty is sufficient in itself, but it warms the soul and sets the atmosphere in which we find it so much easier to be restored in our love-relationship with Christ. A splendid Christian book may be an instrument of blessing, or simply meditating on the Scriptures, or just digesting what one has heard and read over recent months. And there is time to converse with the Lord.

Such times away are also necessary for re-setting our navigation – of seeing what is important and what is secondary. After Jesus was apart in Mark 1 He did not return to the crowd around Peter's house but altered course: 'I must go to other cities also.' For us the rush and activity of life often mean that we cease to see the wood for the trees. We get hurt by comments or criticisms but here apart we can see them in perspective – particularly that we are, in the end, answerable to the Lord for our life and not to man. When others tell us that they are praying for us to be like someone else and have their gifts (or when we wish this ourselves) we need to stand back and realise that we are called to run the race set before *us* and not before someone else. Vision and direction can be wonderfully renewed for us by such times apart and our eyes lifted beyond and above the task to Jesus himself.

Then we Need the refilling of the Holy Spirit. This must be our daily desire, but we will particularly pray for his refilling after times of tiredness and busy-ness, and as we rise afresh to face what lies ahead. This is notably demonstrated to us in Acts 4.31, where the bruised and battered disciples throw themselves on their sovereign Lord and seek the refilling of the Spirit in order to speak the Word of God with boldness. In I Corinthians 12.13 we are told that 'by one Spirit we were all baptised into one body' – the initiatory act of the Spirit – but then, 'and made to drink of one Spirit.' Drink is something in the physical realm that has to be taken day by day – we cannot take enough water to last us a month. So in Christ we need to drink of the Spirit day by day and in the special times apart need particular refilling to overcome our spiritual dehydration, desiring to grow in the fruit of the Spirit and seeking his gifting for the tasks ahead. We do not want simply to *feel* renewed; we want to *be* restored, renewed, refilled and ready to go on for our Lord, being more fruitful in his service and deepened in the privilege of abiding in him and he in us – the privilege of the supreme love-relationship, into which he brought us and which goes on for ever.

Let Charles Wesley express this prayer and hope:

> 'Finish then thy new creation,
> Pure and spotless let us be:
> Let us see thy great salvation
> Perfectly restored in thee.
>
> Changed from glory into glory,
> Till in heaven we take our place;
> Till we cast our crowns before thee,
> Lost in wonder, love and praise.'

SECTION THREE

INTERCESSION

13   PRAYER IN THE BATTLE

The biggest surprise most of us will have when we get to heaven will be in seeing, from that perspective, the scope and intensity of the spiritual battle. We are so often like soldiers in a war-time battle who are told that the enemy is attacking forcibly but do little about it and so are over-run and defeated.

Ephesians 6.18-20 is a key passage for understanding the scope of intercession. 'Pray at all times in the Spirit, with all prayer and supplication. To that end keep alert with all perseverance, making supplication for all the saints, and also for me, that utterance may be given me in opening my mouth boldly to proclaim the mystery of the gospel'. The passage forms the basis of most of this section of the book. But see its context. From verse 10 onwards it is the context of *battle* – being strong in the Lord, putting on the whole armour of God, standing against the wiles of the devil, contending against the spiritual hosts of wickedness.

You can only win the spiritual battle with the right weapons. You cannot stop a radio-wave with a fly-swat; you cannot stop a bullet with a plastic raincoat; you cannot stop a laser beam with a piece of cardboard; and you cannot stop the evil one without spiritual armour and the spiritual weapons of the Word and prayer, or, as old English put it, 'the weapon of all-prayer'. Churches and Christian groups which do not see the necessity of intercessory prayer might as well close their doors now – they will be defeated.

Prayer takes the spiritual battle seriously and 'means business' with the Lord of all power and might. There are five marks of real prayer, or 'prayer in the Spirit,' as Ephesians 6.18 puts it.

1 ACCURATE

Vague waffling prayer is a waste of breath and time. Prayer needs to be on target. Often we can discern that target and can get praying, but sometimes it is not so clear how to pray for a particular situation, even though we realize that prayer is vital in it.

Here the Spirit is ready to help us and direct us. As Romans 8.26 puts it: 'the Spirit helps us in our weakness; for we do not know how to pray as we ought, but the Spirit himself intercedes for us with sighs too deep for words'. That can be the experience in personal intercession: a deep burden of the Spirit that comes upon us, and which causes us to lift that burden to the Lord. It can be similar in corporate intercession, when suddenly a topic comes 'on fire' – there is a movement of the Spirit burdening the group for a person or an event, and all other topics are temporarily dropped as we concentrate on this one thing. As James Montgomery's hymn says: 'Prayer is the soul's sincere desire, uttered or unexpressed, the motion of a hidden fire that trembles in the breast'.

The Spirit can help us to focus on a particular aspect of a mission enterprise 10,000 miles away, burdening us with the right praying for that moment; he can draw our hearts at any time of day or night to pray and only after many months do we learn how that fitted in to God's plan and how we were part of a prayer force vital for an intense part of the spiritual battle. How often we will learn from a missionary or someone else serving God that they were conscious of being supported in a special way, given the right words to speak in a difficult moment or delivered from danger, at the same time as we were burdened to pray.

As we pray through our lists of intercessions, individually or with others, let us keep alert to the Spirit's prompting that we may be accurate in prayer.

2 FERVENT

James 5.16-18 says, 'The prayer of a righteous man has great power in its effects. Elijah was a man of like nature with ourselves and he prayed fervently that it might not rain, and for three years and six months it did not rain on the earth. Then he prayed again and the heaven gave rain and the earth brought forth its fruit'. Some praying! What then is 'fervently' here? For many people it is assumed to mean a special voice of trembling or intensity. Prayer expressed 'with emotion' is regarded by them as the only effective prayer, and straightforward speaking to God is dismissed as 'not fervent prayer'. It is an inaccurate interpretation and an unhelpful viewpoint. What the Greek says here is 'with prayer he prayed'. Nothing about a trembling voice but obviously meaning that he meant business with God – his prayer was real and from the heart. He really *prayed*, whether with or without an emotional voice is immaterial.

When we come to pray, it must not be empty words or an outward facade. Prayer in a service or a prayer gathering which seems more for the human hearers than for God to hear is off centre, like the prayer described as 'the most eloquent prayer ever offered to a Boston congregation'. Prayer is to God, from the heart, with reality. This is fervency, and prayer without such fervency is not prayer. The disciples found themselves helpless in dealing with the demoniac boy in Mark 9.29. Was it that they 'used' prayer as a formula for healing but did not really come in fervent prayer to God? Is this why Jesus says 'this kind cannot be driven out by anything but prayer (and fasting)'?

I ask myself: 'Is my interceding always with such fervency? Or do I let my prayers become a recital, a routine rather than looking to the Lord? Do our prayer gatherings seek to maintain this God-centred, God-dependent fervency?

3 EXPECTANT

James 1 verse 6 Say 'Ask in faith, with no doubting, for he who doubts is like a wave of the sea that is driven and tossed by the wind. For that person must not suppose that a double-minded man, unstable in all his ways, will receive anything from the Lord.'

Expectancy is, of course, submitted to the foundations of prayer in the purposes and ways of God, but it is still to be a real mark of praying, not least that God is always *able* to do more than we ask or think. This then rules out of court the sort of tentative praying that is mentioning a matter because something might happen, but we cannot see how and we don't really expect to receive an answer – and so we don't!

On the other hand, submitting our requests to the will and plans of God will protect us from the immature, mechanical view of this phrase 'Ask in faith' which one sometimes hears! 'I pray for Debbie – I pray with faith – I claim her for Christ', or, 'I pray in faith for my parents, my brothers and sisters – that they may all be converted, by the end of the month.' We take time to learn the place of prayer in the midst of the battle, not least over people turning to Christ.

However, expectancy, with the humble 'your will be done, O Lord', is a mark of real prayer. When we come to special evangelistic services in our churches it is not much use praying without expectancy – and we will learn to pray 'on target' for spiritual blindness to be removed, for power in testimony and the ministry of the Word and for the Holy Spirit to be moving amongst us. We must expect God to bring *his* results, which may be to move a lot of people a step nearer the Kingdom, rather than a few people actually coming to Christ. Expect and on that occasion trust the Lord to know what is best.

Expectancy can also be a growing conviction. We may face up to a venture for the Lord or some particular challenge. As we pray – perhaps over a period of weeks or months – we begin to sense that 'the Lord is in this'. There are encouraging signs of our being 'on track' and in line with his will. So our expectancy increases and we begin to have the faith in God that believes mountains can be removed. (Mark 11.24)

4 EARNEST

When Peter was in prison 'earnest prayer for him was made to God by the church'. (Acts 12.5) What does 'earnest' mean? Again, some people put it in the emotion-in-the-voice category, but the original word actually has the sense of laying hands on someone and thus identifying with them. So, as the group of Christians prayed for Peter they, in a sense, identified with him, lifting him up to the Lord together with love, urgency and deep oneness. When a person in special need is with us in a prayer gathering some of us may lay hands on his head, as a representative identification of the group and an outward sign of our inward 'earnestness' in prayer for them. In the same way, in our personal intercessions, it is good to try and identify with the person for whom we are praying – with what they are feeling and facing.

But there is also earnestness towards God. We see this with Jesus in Gethsemane. As Luke 22 records it: 'And being in an agony he prayed more *earnestly*; and his sweat became as drops of blood falling to the ground.' Here, in a sense, Jesus is 'laying hands' on his Father, reaching out to him, deeply identifying with the Father's will, in spite of the enormous burden of Calvary ahead. There are those who seem specially called out as deep intercessors – warriors of prayer, with that ability to come earnestly to the Lord. There are times too when God calls us to spend days or nights in prayer together as a church or as groups (as Jesus did before choosing the twelve). Those who have shared in extended times of prayer like this know how, after a while, the reality of meeting with the Lord seems to deepen and prayer itself takes on the richer depth of earnestness.

5 PERSEVERING

The fifth mark comes from Ephesians 6 .18 itself: 'To this end keep alert with all perseverance'. We often have to persevere in prayer because we cannot see what is happening in the spiritual realm. Daniel 10 is an example of this. When Daniel has spent three weeks of prayer and fasting the heavenly messenger tells him that his prayer was heard from the beginning but 'the prince of the kingdom of Persia withstood me twenty-one days'.

We shall never fully understand how our prayers are effective in the spiritual battle – nor how our prayers are involved in God's will and action. But it is clear from

Scripture that they *are*, and this is why we must press on in persevering prayer – perhaps over many years – when we know that the matter has been laid on our hearts by the Holy Spirit. We must trust God's timings. Here is someone who prays for forty years for his son to come to faith and dies without seeing the answer. The son is actually brought to Christ through his father's funeral! Here is a small group of Christians in an area that seems dead spiritually. The ministers of the local churches seem to have grown cold spiritually. The flame of the Gospel seems almost extinguished. But the group sets itself to pray and to persevere. Eventually the impossible happens. A new minister is appointed who is spiritually alive and the Kingdom of God begins to grow in that area. Here are many who persevere in prayer for the Muslim world, or for Jews, or for other religious groups that seem very resistant towards the Gospel. The burden is laid on their hearts to pray. How much they must have perseverance. Here is another group facing a venture for Christ. Their expectancy has grown and they are sure they are in the Lord's will but the obstacles come one by one – and they have to pray for God's solution and over-ruling, time and time again. The battle is all the way and they must not grow tired. They are called to persevering prayer.

Martin Luther said, 'To pray diligently is more than half the task'. We may not always understand the how and the why of prayer but two things *are* clear – the disaster of no-prayer and the power of real prayer. We wrestle against the powers of spiritual darkness, but we wrestle in the power of God as we join in 'battle prayer' with accuracy, fervency, expectancy, earnestness and perseverance. 'Pray at all times in the Spirit, with all prayer and supplication.'

14 PRAYER AT ALL TIMES

There are many times and ways for intercessory prayer to take place. Let us think our way through a number of them:

1 THE BREATH OF PRAYER

The habit of lifting our hearts in intercession at any time of day or night is a valuable way of spreading the coverage of prayer. We are about to write a letter or make a telephone call – can we pause and lift what we write or say to the Lord? We are about to have an interview with an employer, or we are about to do the interviewing – can we pause to pray? We are setting out on a journey, perhaps setting off on holiday as a family. Can we pause to pray? We are sitting in a bus or an Underground train. Our eyes can go along the bus or train praying for our fellow-passengers. We are crammed into a lift, riding up to the seventeenth floor. We can pray for the other people in the lift. We are reading the newspaper, listening to the news on the radio or watching the news on television. We can turn our minds to God in prayer, lifting up to him people with colossal responsibility in leadership or people caught in some disaster or the relatives of people killed in a plane crash. Once we begin to 'breathe prayer' there is no limit to our intercession.

2 INTERCESSION ALONE

Interceding alone does not seem as readily practicable as we would like to make out. Some years ago I had to produce a paper on 'Spirituality' for a group of ministers and did some practical research by means of anonymous question-naires and in gathering small groups of Christians who would be honest with me about their spiritual lives. I found the amount of time spent in intercession by the ministers far less than I would have imagined. Then, with a group of outstanding Christian laymen, all influential leaders in the local church, I was staggered to find that though all of them kept a regular time each day for devotional prayer – in approach to God for the new day – *none* of them had daily times of intercession for others. It is not possible to assess how general is this state of affairs but I suspect it may be far more general than we would like to believe.

The reason seems partly a matter of time, partly a matter that intercessory prayer is easier in a group (and all of the laymen I spoke to were regular intercessors at the church prayer gathering) and partly a matter of system. It may be that the burden of personal intercessors is to be on those who have more time – the elderly or those laid aside with illness (although often those who are ill find it difficult to pray). Many retired people are marvellous intercessors and I am often embarrassed by (though thankful for) the care with which they support one's ministry and the life of the Church at home and abroad. I know I cannot match that but it does not let me out of intercessory responsibility. There are times when one can give oneself more fully to intercession and in a recent time in hospital for an operation I found great joy in being able to intercede without limitation of time. Yet I must find time in my normal daily life. It may be separate from my devotional approach to God, or the two may come together.

So what about a system? Naturally we will need no system to pray daily for our family, ourselves and others who are close to us. We carry them close to our heart. However, we may find it difficult to be fresh in prayer and the suggestion made earlier in the book (under 'Worship') that we take a fresh thought from our reading of the Scriptures and use it in prayer can be the answer. It is, of course, an idea we can carry across all our intercession that day. So if, for instance, the text 'You will keep him in perfect peace whose mind is stayed on you' has blessed our hearts that morning then we could pray for that staying of the mind on the Lord and its consequent peace for ourselves, and the members of our family, colleagues, missionaries and so on. The next day the Word to our hearts might be on spiritual growth – and this will be our particular prayer concern for ourselves and others. Thus each day our regular praying is fresh.

Beyond our immediate family and friends, some system is necessary if we are to cover the many needs for prayer. Here we need to have a good loose-leaf notebook. The first page could be for daily prayer, but it is doubtful whether we need a list, as these people and concerns will be on our hearts. We might find it helpful though to paste in some written prayers which could be a help to us.

Next we need to organize the coverage of the week. We must decide whether to make this a seven-day coverage or perhaps a six or five-day coverage – leaving Sunday out, as we shall be gathering with others and though we will spend time preparing for worship we could say that intercession will be in the services. Others will say that Sunday is *the* day for their intercession as they have more time – so work out your own way!. Some may leave out Saturday as a 'day off'. Once we have settled the days we must settle our use of the days. I find it difficult to move instantly from praying, say, for South America, to praying for the elderly of the parish and then for a mission in the inner city. For me the 'breakthrough' came when I 'went thematic'. Each of my intercessory days was assigned its theme – on Monday for all those working with me in the total life of the local church and for the sections of the church's life; on Tuesday for all missionaries and world mission and world leaders; on Wednesday for the wider range of my family, friends, people for whom I have a particular spiritual responsibility and for all those new to faith; on Thursday for the wide range of people known to me who are in Christian ministry or in 'secular' occupations with effective influence for Christ; on Friday for a range of Christian organizations involved in evangelism, outreach, social work, relief of world need, the arts and so on; on Saturday, for all that is to take place on the Sunday. The liberty this gave me was that if on a particular day I felt I could not face a list of topics and names, I could still give myself freely to praying on the theme of the day, open to the Spirit's leading. It meant too that some names or needs on the lists would become special targets for prayer as the Spirit touched one's heart. It is a system that has not 'gone cold' on me though I have used it for many years.

Alongside the weekly pattern we shall obviously pray each day for the particular events of that day in our church's programme – for the classes of new believers, youth groups and so on.

We have a monthly pattern church diary in our parish that I use as well. This covers our missionaries and world mission on one side of the page across the thirty days and every aspect of our church's work and its leaders on the other side. This gives particular concentration of prayer. To this monthly list can be added the names of people we want to pray for whom we cannot 'handle' in the scope of weekly prayer.

Clearly we cannot pray for everyone and every need we see or hear about. Parts of world mission will be particularly on our hearts for prayer and we shall try to keep our praying informed. It would be impossible to do that for the whole world. The same selectivity is obviously necessary over the whole panorama of prayer.

One other page is often added. This is for a prayer for short-term needs – perhaps a specific event or opportunity or exam. This page requires frequent re-writing but does help us fulfil our promises, so readily made, to pray for people when they ask us to do so.

3 INTERCESSION IN TWOS AND THREES

The promise of the Lord in Matthew 18.19 is that 'if two of you agree on earth about anything they ask, it will be done for them by my Father in heaven. For where two or three are gathered in my name, there am I in the midst of them'. Why should prayer in two's and three's be more effective? Perhaps the answer is that together we can sense more accurately when we are praying 'on target' through the Lord's promised presence with us.

For many Christians intercessory prayer is more normally in such a 'group' of two or three than alone. Some married couples share in this way. Some friends do, particularly if sharing a house or flat. At my theological college there was a 'prayer partnership' scheme. You joined it voluntarily and it meant your spending some time with a different fellow-student each week, in prayer. It meant praying some weeks with men you did not readily like, but often when you met together to pray, real understanding developed.

It is 'natural' to the Christian life to pray together after a counselling session or when we have had an evening together in a home or even before parting at a street corner. We will pray together when visiting in hospital or visiting a sick person at home or when we have shared a problem together. When Paul said farewell to the Ephesian elders in Acts 20.36 they knelt, prayed, wept and embraced. It is 'natural' to Christian fellowship.

4 INTERCESSION IN THE BODY – THE PRAYER GATHERING

I can understand the hesitancy of some people about open prayer gatherings. They regard them as 'super-spiritual' events and may describe them as 'holy huddles' not for the likes of them! I had the same feelings when I was a youth. Then one morning on the way to work I made a careless mistake. The leader of the Youth Group said: 'See you at the P.M. on Saturday, Michael?' I am never very good at initials, especially in the morning, and I mistook 'P.M.' for 'Y.F.' (Youth Fellowship). So I said 'yes'. Then I realized what I had said. P.M. stood for prayer meeting! My youthful pride conflicted with my fear. Pride won and I turned up for the prayer meeting. Only two others were there. We knelt in the front room of the house, each one at a chair. Mine was a deep-blue velvet-covered arm-chair. I remember it vividly! The other two (girls) prayed fluently and at length. Then there was a long, long silence! The sweat broke out on my forehead and streamed down my face. It then dripped on to the blue velvet! Eventually I stuttered out some sort of prayer. However, mercifully it did not frighten me off for life, but made me ask myself why I should get into such a lather about praying to God aloud, as I had no difficulty praying in silence nor talking aloud to others about anything and everything!

So, if you are a new Christian, don't avoid the prayer gathering (it will usually be much larger than three and you won't usually be embarrassed – others will pray if you are silent). It will widen the scope of your praying. You will learn from others and be helped to pray for many people and needs, agreeing in your mind with the one leading in prayer. Then you may find it helpful to write out a prayer and to 'break the ice' of opening your mouth in a prayer gathering by reading it aloud. To move on to extempore praying, you will need to have the Lord firmly at the centre of your praying, and forget about the other people present (what does it matter what they think?). If there are those who use 'thou', 'wast', 'hath' and so on, don't copy them. Use today's English. There is no special holiness in Elizabethan language and it can get you in a tangle. God expects us to pray straight, and from the heart. For most of us that will be in the language of the present day and without undue length.

The prayer gathering whatever form it takes is of key importance in the life of a church. It is never to be an 'optional extra' to the week or just one event among many. It must have the best night of the week and nothing else must go on in the church's programme on that night. In All Souls it is every other Tuesday. We have established a pattern of meeting all together on one Tuesday and then in Fellowship Groups on the next. The fellowship groups concentrate on Bible study and sharing personal prayer needs, as well as friendship and support. The prayer gathering concentrates on praise and prayer, particularly for the Church's work and for world mission. All leaders are expected to be at the prayer gathering and to give it top priority. All the church family is urged to be present.

The pattern of our meeting has been carefully worked out. Before the actual gathering, there is an opportunity to eat together or have a coffee. Then, for the meeting itself, the seating is set as closely as possible in concentric circles to aid audibility and create a sense of being together.

We begin with worship, leading into praise and thanksgiving. We ask that praises should be brief – phrases, sentences but not paragraphs. This enables a lot of people to share in thanking and praising. Normally we remain standing and sing to start and end this section.

Then we may have a brief thought from the Scriptures – a key-note for praying. This is followed by a collated list of prayer needs and topics. Time is taken over explaining these needs so that we can later be 'agreed' in prayer for them. Sometimes there is an urgent or special need we take first. Often different leaders or members will mention briefly needs of their group or of a person. In the case of healing prayer we may ask the person to come into the centre so that we can hear from them first-hand and lay hands on as we pray. Around the room the needs are then taken up in prayer. we encourage 'conversational' prayer, that is, spending time on a topic, with several prayers for it or prayers that lead naturally across to a similar need. We discourage lengthy praying. At times a particular theme comes 'on fire' and the spirit leads us to concentrate at length on it. Quite often we have a time at the end of this section when we say a name of a person, mention a need or an event, without starts or ends – this is particularly helpful for those who find it difficult to frame a longer prayer. We often then pray in silence for those next to us so that everyone present is prayed for.

A time of small-group prayer usually follows, but not always. We turn our chairs into groups of five or six and either pray for one or two special topics, such as the next evangelistic service, or for needs of people in the group. It is not over-long, so as to avoid embarrassment to those not able to articulate prayers. We bring it to an end with the piano being played to introduce a hymn.

The final section is normally on world mission. If we have a missionary home we will obviously focus this time on him or her and the work in which they are involved. At other times we will cover a particular area of the world, or concentrate on a work of outreach or relief. We end with a hymn, followed by quite a number of relaxed notices in the family atmosphere, after which people stay on to meet and share fellowship. The meeting itself is one and a half hours. It is the hub of our life and work at All Souls.

5 INTERCESSION IN THE BODY – IN CHURCH SERVICES

Is the intercessory part of a service the 'low' part for us, a moment when our mind wanders off? Is it too formal in liturgical services and too world-roving in non-liturgical services? It certainly ought to be a vital part of the service, involving the congregation with 'agreement' in prayer. This could be helped by different people leading, by those who lead giving very careful preparation, by so fitting into the theme of the service that the prayers have a fresh 'angle' each week, by congregational response after each item of prayer, by extempore prayer from the congregation if the church is fairly small, or by several people deputed to lead from the congregation. An overhead projector showing a map or a drawing can 'lift' prayer concentration. The occasional 'visual prayer', when we project colour slides and pray for the need portrayed by each one, can be refreshing. To a large extent the key lies with the person leading and the time and thought they give to this important part of the service, but the rest of the congregation must make a conscious resolve not just to listen but to pray.

6 SPECIAL TIMES OF PRAYER

The New Testament gives us several examples of the church having special gatherings for prayer, as in the setting apart of Saul and Barnabas, or for Peter in prison. When as a church or a Christian group we are facing special challenges we should meet them with special prayer. This will be true in a venture of faith such as a building project, or in a time of particular opposition to the Gospel in our area, or as we have a mission or have to make some big decision. We may call the church together for an evening of prayer, a day of prayer, or a night of prayer. We may arrange a series of special gatherings and ask those who cannot come to pray where they are at that time (e.g. in the early morning).

7 S.O.S. PRAYER

This is urgent prayer that often cannot wait for a meeting to be arranged. It is a call from a member of the fellowship or part of the church's 'extended' family elsewhere in the country or overseas. Often it will be about a sudden illness, a matter of life-and-death, or some devastating blow or threat. Here we will often telephone around various friends and fellow-members of the church asking them for S.O.S. prayer. Separately (and together when possible) the fellowship has to rush into action, lifting the person or persons on to the prayer stretcher and bringing them to the feet of the Lord. It is literally a matter of 'stop – and pray'.

8 SPECIAL SUPPORT

A friend may be facing a tough day or a tough week, an exam, difficult decisions, an operation, or speaking at a conference. If possible, try to remind yourself to keep lifting them to the Lord through the day or through the week. I am grateful to my wife for praying when I am speaking, even when I am in a different time-zone of the world, and I am equally grateful to the numerous other members of the church who do the same. It is a privilege of Christian fellowship to receive and give this special prayer support.

9 SEEING A SPIRITUAL NEED

When we see a *material* need, we are to meet it by action and giving if possible. When we see a *spiritual* need we should meet it with action and praying. So in 1 John 5.16: 'If any one sees his brother committing what is not a mortal sin, he will ask and God will give him life …' Older Christians can often see the dangers facing younger Christians. The younger are often confident but older

Christians were once young and have remarkable memories! They can see the mistakes being made and know the possible consequences. They may not feel that any advice from them will be received but they can pray. Peter 'couldn't be told' about his impending failure of denial, so Jesus prayed for him that his faith would not fail. Such a spiritual alertness and prayerfulness is not confined to the older members – it is part of Christian fellowship and love for us all. The effects of such prayer can be of eternal consequence.

15   PRAYER FOR THE SAINTS

Ephesians 6:18 speaks of 'Making supplication for all the saints.' The description of all those who belong to God as 'saints' is used more than sixty times in the New Testament. The less exact modern usage – e.g. 'I'm no saint' – has devalued the biblical concept of 'the Lord's people' as those who belong to his family for ever, his saints! Paul's command to pray 'for all the saints' puts upon us a responsibility of special prayer support for the whole of the Lord's family here on earth and particularly for all those we know in it. This love and prayer-care for fellow believers is well demonstrated by Paul himself. He writes, for instance, to the Thessalonians: 'We give thanks to God always for you all, constantly mentioning you in our prayers'.

For us this will mean praying for fellow-members of our church or Christian group and Christians we know elsewhere or who have gone overseas in service. Most will no doubt go on our monthly prayer list so that we can pray more specifically for them, but we will also want to lift some to the Lord as occasion arises. What do we pray? 'Bless Pat', 'Bless Jim'? or is there more to it? There are three aspects of prayer for fellow-Christians in the New Testament which may guide us in our praying for them – but, as we also are saints through faith in Christ, we should pray the same for ourselves.

1 SPIRITUALLY

It is natural to pray first for our own or our fellow-Christians' safety, well-being, health or success. However, if we read through the prayers of the New Testament we find them overwhelmingly concerned with the spiritual growth of believers. So that must be our priority.

Ephesians 3.14-19 – gives us one such prayer. It is a magnificent expression of heartfelt praying. It is a prayer for the Ephesians to know increasing spiritual power, in terms of the riches of God's glory and not of meagre human expectation. How much we need to pray this. We have been born anew by the Holy Spirit, brought into the spiritual dimension of living, but we can then so easily be content with a mediocre spiritual standard, lacking the boldness of witness and not having an increasing victory in the fight against 'the world, the flesh and the devil'. In our own strength we will fail. Only by the increasing might of the Holy Spirit can we go forward.

This leads into a prayer that 'Christ may dwell in your hearts through faith'. The Holy Spirit glorifies Christ. It follows that a person full of the Holy Spirit will not be Spirit-centred but Christ-centred. The Holy Spirit strengthens us and we find ourselves closer to Christ, saying, with Paul, 'I can do all things in Christ who strengthens me'. The letter to the Philippians hardly mentions the Holy Spirit but is full of Christ – yet Paul is clearly filled with the Holy Spirit. Again, the Spirit opens up to us what Christ means by 'Abide in me and I in you'.

Then the prayer is concerned with the fruit of Christian character, that the Ephesians will be rooted and grounded in love – knowing the deep security of the covenant-love relationship but also the fruitful growth in love, joy, peace, patience, kindness, goodness, faithfulness, gentleness and self-control – the forming of the character of Christ in us. There is no limit to such growth, no point where we can say we have arrived. So we pray that we and other Christians may go on discovering more and more of the breadth, length, height and depth of the glorious love of God – a love which can overwhelm us and which we can experience in such reality that it goes beyond knowledge.

The aim of the prayer is that believers may be filled with the fullness of God – not content with second-rate Christian living – always wanting to grow at whatever age. One of the marks of spiritual life in elderly Christians is that, however old they are, they want to learn more of Christ and to grow in him. There is no retirement. As the outward fabric decays, the inner nature goes on being renewed day by day.

Just before I left Manchester, a new bishop was appointed to the diocese. There was a big service in the cathedral and then a great reception in the grandeur of the town hall. All the clergy were invited and various civic leaders. The tables were laid out with all sorts of food but, being polite Englishmen, we had our cups of tea and took a few of the delicately-cut cucumber sandwiches. However, there was one little old lady there – I do not know how she came to be present – who was obviously living on a small income. She was not going to miss the opportunity of this occasion. Elbowing clergy out of her way, she tackled the goodies (ignoring the polite sandwiches) with gusto. At one point, faced with a bowl in which large segments of pineapple lay awash in juice, she looked for a spoon, but, not seeing one, plunged her hand into the bowl to get the pineapple out. We continued with our polite cucumber sandwiches!

Are we like that over spiritual things – content with our polite form of respectable Christianity and almost despising those who seem to be 'too keen' for our liking? Or are we prepared to see 'the riches of his glory' laid out for his people and so begin to hunger for more of our Lord's provision for us, thrusting our hand into the bowl and growing in his fullness? No need for spiritual slimming; growth is the aim.

So let us pray this prayer, as it stands in Ephesians 3, or the main thrust of it, for ourselves and for our fellow-Christians – for our pastors, leaders and all who serve, for new Christians, for older Christians who may start to have a spiritual 'middle-age-spread' of slowing up, for elderly believers that their lives may be a rich testimony to the fruits of spiritual growth.

In the New Testament we also learn to pray for spiritual protection for fellow-Christians. Jesus shows this to us when, in Luke 22.32, he prays for Peter. Satan, he says, is going to 'sift' Peter. Note that Jesus does not pray for the attack not to happen but that Peter's faith will not fail and that afterwards he will strengthen his brethren. Those of us who are parents or youth leaders may long that teenagers could avoid the pressures that come upon them in growing

103

up, the temptation to swing away from Christ and to conform to the world. Yet they have to face that stage of life. We do not pray that they should avoid it, but that they will come through it with faith, not only intact, but growing. We would apply the same prayer policy to fellow Christians facing problems, illness or bereavement. Although we will pray for them in their physical need, we will have a primary prayer-aim of seeing them come through with deepened faith and the ability to help others facing similar situations in the future. It is the spiritual nature which is eternal. The physical is only temporary. So spiritual growth is a prime target for prayer.

2 MENTALLY

In ordinary life we know the limitations of understanding and of coping with life that come when a young person cannot be bothered to work or learn at school, even as a 'one-talent' person. Later in life so many kick themselves for having lost out on the opportunities they had available to them. On the other hand, you can see the way in which those who do work and study, according to their abilities, grow in confidence in tackling the whole of life. The principles of understanding and learning open up all sorts of avenues and life can go on being enriched.

It is similar in the Christian life. By faith in Christ we are brought into fellowship with God, the fount of all wisdom and truth. The Holy Spirit indwells us as the interpreter of the wisdom of God. There is no limit to growth in understanding the things of God, whatever our abilities. Naturally, the ten-talent intellect is expected to grow in spiritual understanding appropriately and the one-talent not so much, but growth is expected in both. Yet so often, like some school-children, Christians 'cannot be bothered'. They sit lightly to sermons, to teaching in groups and to Christian books. Their bookcase reflects their lack of desire to grow in understanding – often it only has a collection of the more 'sensational' Christian paperbacks. They lack confidence in the Christian life because of so much basic ignorance and because what they believe has not been thought through in any depth. On the other hand, the Christian who wants to grow in his understanding can do so if he has access to books and is prepared to listen and think. People whose intellectual ability is quite small can make significant growth; it is not limited to the highly intelligent, though they are rightly expected to go further in using the minds they have been given. I have seen people come to Christ who have been unable to read or write, but who have longed to grow and so have learnt to read and write and then go on reading; others who have never read a book in their life have found the Holy Spirit helping them to read and understand, because they wanted to grow. It involves discipline, determination and that desire to grow on our part. The Holy Spirit matches that with his opening of our understanding. In all who grow like this there comes an increasing confidence in the Christian life, an increased ability to communicate the faith to others, and a deepening richness in understanding the things of God.

Paul is sufficiently concerned about such growth to make it a matter of prayer for the saints. In Philippians 1.9, for instance, he prays that 'your love may abound more and more, with knowledge and all discernment, so that you may approve what is excellent ... and may be pure and blameless ... filled with the fruits of righteousness.'

Sometimes there seems to be almost a despising of Christian understanding. People who say, 'Your faith is too cerebral' may be rightly rejecting a coldly intellectual approach, but often they seem to be simply anti-intellectual. The pendulum swings into experience without understanding. The New Testament is much more balanced. As Paul shows us in Philippians 1.9, love is to abound more and more, but with knowledge and all discernment. Experience and understanding go warmly hand in hand. We need them both. The gifts to the Church, in Ephesians 4, are to bring us 'to the unity of the faith and of the knowledge of the Son of God, to mature manhood, to the measure of the stature of the fulness of Christ'. And the reason? So that we may not be like children, 'tossed to and fro and carried about by every wind of doctrine'. There will be stability but not coldness, for it continues: 'Rather, speaking the truth in love ...'

We are all under pressure to 'conform to the world'. The media powerfully influences us. Transformation is 'by the renewal of your mind'. (Romans 12.2) There is a battle for the mind, and the young Christian is in the thick of the battle. He particularly needs prayer, but so do all of us. Some seem to 'give up without a fight' and get lost. Some opt out into authoritarian groups which do the 'thinking' for them.

May we always want to grow in our Christian understanding – reading, thinking, taking notes, learning. We must pray it for ourselves! But we must also pray it for our Christian friends, that the church's teachers and preachers may not stop learning, fossilising in middleage, but may go on growing in their discernment and understanding; for the young people that they may not just grow in understanding in their academic subjects but may use their minds to grow into Christian adulthood; that those without much intellectual capacity may not give up but may long to grow too; that day by day or in mid-week Bible study groups, when our friends open the Scriptures they may see new things as the Holy Spirit interprets; that for Sunday's preaching the preacher might find his understanding wonderfully opened up in preparation and the congregation responding to the preaching itself with stimulated minds, warm hearts and responsive action; that friends in the Christian 'front-line' may have wisdom to know how to speak for Christ and uphold his truth; that Christians involved in broadcasting, television, writing and the arts may grow in understanding as they seek to communicate. The range of such prayer is widespread. So let us pray, that in terms of 1 Corinthians 14.20 the saints may 'not be children in thinking', but 'in thinking be mature'.

3 PHYSICALLY

We pray readily for physical well-being in our lives and in the lives of fellow-Christians, because pain, suffering, danger, hunger, tension and illness affect our bodies, and our bodies react! So we can feel for other people in their suffering or problems and we long to help them. Prayer is one way we can do so.

Our hearts will be lifted up in prayer for Christians suffering persecution, deprivation and imprisonment. Physical help is often limited. Spiritual help is unlimited. Prayer is not stopped by the bars of a prison cell. Then there are the many Christians in refugee camps and in areas of the world where food supplies are desperately inadequate. Here our physical help in terms of money and supplies is more possible, but the roots of the problem go much deeper and can only be touched through prayer. We will want to pray for those trying to tackle the problems on the spot.

It is natural also to pray for one another in the journeyings of life, whether to the local shopping centre, or across the world by plane. How often we can see the Lord's hand in events, yet how much more will we see this when we look back on our life from the heavenly perspective and see what has been prevented, without our knowing anything about it.

However, the question of healing is the major concern to most Christians when thinking about prayer for physical well-being. So we will concentrate on it.

The key to all prayer for healing is in the glory of God. If we accept the foundations of prayer which we discussed in Section I of this book, then the glory of God will be our greatest concern and we will submit all healing prayer to that higher purpose. Hallesby, in his classic book on prayer, mentions Samuel Zeller, who lived years ago in Switzerland. Zeller was a great speaker, pastor and pray-er. Through him many were healed. Yet Zeller never prayed just for healing but for God to be glorified. He would add to healing prayer: 'If it will glorify thy name more, then let them remain sick, but, if that be thy will, give them power to glorify thy name through their illness'. That was courageous but accurate praying and in no way minimised his effectiveness as an instrument of healing. Many were healed; but many were not healed. His prayer for the Lord's glory was from the heart. Perhaps it was for that same glory that he himself had an ailment all his life.

There is immense damage to people, to Christian integrity and to the Lord's honour from those who teach that *all* illnesses can and should be healed, and that as illness is a mark of the fallen sinful world, God can only be glorified in healing, not in permitting sickness to be for his purposes of glory. The argument often cites Matthew 8.17 and its reference to Isaiah 53 to claim that, on the Cross, Christ carried our sicknesses as well as our sins. If that means physical wholeness for the believer on the one hand, it must mean spiritual perfection on the other. But although we have the power of Christ, we still have mortal bodies and fallen natures until we die. Triumphs and victories take place, but the perfect wholeness is in heaven.

The results of 'all can be healed' teaching bring some people to despair because they are not healed and so presume it is due to sin in their life or lack of faith. It brings others into deception, claiming they are healed even though they are quite clearly in the same physical state as before. A godly doctor friend told me this: 'A dear Christian lady patient developed multiple sclerosis of rapid and severe character. She told me that the Lord was going to heal her and she had profound faith. In process of time she was getting steadily worse and one day said that she considered my lack of faith was the obstacle. It happened that a lady healer was visiting the town. I arranged ambulance and wheel chair for my patient to be present at the healing service. Hands were laid upon her and she claimed to be "cured". Sadly, in fact the disease progressed to a fatal termination but she never again blamed me for obstructing her cure'.

The deception can be carried over into books, as the reader does not usually have the opportunity to check the facts. The same lady healer mentioned above wrote a book of her cases of healing, among which was a case which we would call a thalidomide case today. The healing claimed was the replacement of a claw by a new hand. A London surgeon writing a book on healings a few years later said that the healer had been sued by the parents of the child affected, for the child had *not* been healed. However, the surgeon proceeded to justify the lady healer by saying that she had 'seen in her mind's eye' the fingers grow and her faith was so intense that she believed that it had happened.

Others are destroyed in faith when they have believed that all illnesses can and should be cured by prayer and yet it does not happen. We recently received a letter from a house church in South London asking for any cassette tapes on the subject of healing. One of their number had contracted leukaemia. They had prayed with fervency and faith, but the person died. The letter ended with the sad words: 'We have all lost our faith'.

The tragedy is that the balanced biblical view leads to no such problems. To believe in healing prayer (and I do, fervently) yet to submit that to the glory of God, leaves us in trust and peace. This is why the whole first section of this book is about the foundations of prayer. Chapter one is particularly relevant to this discussion on healing.

Paul has it so beautifully sorted out in 2 Corinthians 12. The earlier parts of the letter have shown us how much suffering he had experienced in life. He wrote from first-hand knowledge. In chapter 12.8 he tells us that he pleaded with the Lord three times to take away the 'thorn in my flesh, a messenger of Satan'. God's reply was 'My grace is sufficient for you, for my power is made perfect in weakness'. Thereafter, Paul does not go on praying but accepts the reply and does so not grudgingly but gladly. If this is the way Christ's power is to be upon him then he will *boast* about his weaknesses. For Christ's sake he will *delight* in weaknesses, insults, hardships, persecutions and difficulties. Thus his prayer for healing or deliverance is submitted to the higher purposes of God. The result? No tension, no deception, no destruction of faith, but power and praise! And if it had been God's will to glorify himself through healing deliverance, the result would also have been power and praise!

As Stanley Jones wrote in *Christ and Human Suffering*:

'He told us not to escape suffering but to use it. Christ suggests that we are to take up pain, calamity, injustice and persecution into the purpose of our lives and make them contribute to higher ends, the ends for which we really live. He does not explain suffering or explain it away, but he changed everything. He would turn the world's supreme tragedy into the world's supreme testimony – and did!'

How then do we approach the matter of illness? Do we veer away from healing prayer or come at it in a half-hearted manner? Certainly not. These steps may guide us:

(a) We take hold of faith in the living God and his ability (Ephesians 3.20) to do more than we ask or think. Yes, we believe God is *able* to heal any illness.

(b) We pray – specifically. We will do so, if possible, with other Christians in the context of the church's prayer gathering, or in a service, or in a fellowship group, or at a special gathering of fellow Christians for this purpose. We may lay hands on the person as we pray, identifying ourselves with them, but it is not necessary. At a special gathering we may be able to spend a full evening in prayer. We will want to involve any members of the church who seem to be gifted with healing love and those members who are particularly close to the sick person.

If the person is too ill to come to the fellowship then representatives of the fellowship should go to their bedside, as described in James 5.14.

Prayer will need to be informed, so there must be openness about the nature of the illness. That openness must first be with the sick person, because if relatives are concealing the truth from him or her they will not let the church know and prayer cannot be accurate.

(c) We will appreciate, as James 5.16 in context shows, that there may need to be confession and forgiveness of sin. Harboured grudges or lack of forgiveness can create illness and healing may come when the cause is sorted out.

(d) We will submit our prayers to the purposes of God's glory and will pray as Samuel Zeller did.

(e) We will keep sensitive to the Lord as we pray over weeks or months. Is there a point when he is saying that there is not to be healing (as there was for Paul after 'three times' of pleading)? If so, we will turn our prayer and action even more to supporting the sick person in glorifying the Lord.

How powerfully that can happen in terminal illness! Our sensitivity to the Lord may alternatively guide us to go on praying for healing.

(f) We will be open to the Lord's ways. His healing may be entirely through medical means, or it may be sudden, and we will call it a miracle (though some illnesses are subject to sudden regression). It may be delayed because the Lord wants to bring deep spiritual growth in the time of weakness before restoring the person (as Hudson Taylor and George Muller both experienced).

(g) We will give praise and thanksgiving when we see the Lord has answered for his glory.

(h) We will be sensitive in love to those involved in illness or bereavement where there has been faith and prayer and yet no healing, even though another with a similar illness has been healed.

(i) We will not generalise from the occasional miracle cure to give the impression that everyone can be healed like that. It has been my joy and privilege to see several people suddenly restored to health. The joy has been enormous. God has at times healed exactly at the time the church was praying. I am deeply thankful for these experiences as well as for those where people have been healed and restored more gradually, but in no way could I generalise. I know God can and does heal, so I pray fervently and with faith. I know I must also pray for his glory, in healing or in triumph within the illness, so I submit my prayer to that higher end, and again do so with faith. To God be the glory!

16 PRAYER FOR THE SERVANTS

All servants of God must be saints, but not all saints are servants. We are made saints by God's grace; we become servants by volunteering and surrendering our lives to the Lordship of Christ. Paul was such a servant and asks for prayer support for his task, both in Ephesians 6.18-20 and elsewhere. There is a particular responsibility to pray for those who are involved in the service of Christ, especially where they are in the front-line of battle.

This will mean special prayer support for Christian leaders, pastors, speakers, evangelists and missionaries, but also for one another in our ambassadorship for Christ in our office, factory, college, school, hospital, shop, trade union, work in local or national government, in our trade or in our neighbourhood. Service for Christ is open to all saints and the Lord needs us all.

For what do we pray? Let me suggest five possibilities:

1 FOR BOLDNESS TO SPEAK

Ephesians 6.19: 'Pray also for me, that whenever I open my mouth, words may be given me so that I will fearlessly make known the mystery of the gospel, for which I am an ambassador in chains. Pray that I may declare it fearlessly, as I should.' (NIV) So it was not easy for Paul to witness. That's encouraging, isn't it? He tells the Corinthians how he trembled when he came to them with the gospel. Paul so often seems a 'giant' in the work of the gospel but his strength was not in physical stature but from spiritual renewal. He was obviously thrown back on the Lord constantly, just as Peter and the others were. (Acts 4.31) Get hold of this! We so readily excuse our weaknesses in witnessing by assuming it is easier for other people or that they have an easier situation. But it is never easy to witness and if it ever becomes easy we should stop, because it will have become in *our* strength and abilities and not the Lord's.

We will pray for ourselves as servants that when opportunity comes for witness we may be given courage to speak, not hesitantly or with shame, but powerfully with joy. It is good to commit each day like this. Forcing openings for the gospel is seldom effective, so pray, 'Lord, if you provide the opportunity to speak for you today, I promise I will take it and I pray you will give me boldness and clarity.' Then *keep* the promise. If someone at lunch leads off about 'where is the world going to?' or 'the standards of this country are collapsing – why is it?' or 'I don't reckon there is a God' or any other of the thousands of possible openings, take a deep breath, send up an arrow prayer, open your mouth and speak!

We will want to pray for our close Christian friends that they will have this boldness. We will also pray it for those engaged in projects of evangelism or mission, in evangelistic preaching, in particular situations of witness such as Paul had there in prison and for those Christians in positions of public prominence – in government and national/international leadership. I find it a real experience of the Lord's strength when people pray specially for a broadcast sermon or an evangelistic one. There is no less work in preparation, but one feels carried by the Spirit in preparation and in the speaking.

2 FOR AN OPEN DOOR FOR THE WORD

Colossians 4.2-4: 'Pray for us, too, that God may open a door for our message'. It is one thing to sow the seed; it is another to have ground ready to receive it, where the seed is not choked or trodden down but can take root and flourish.

In evangelistic services, we will need to pray as much for the hearers as for the preacher. Spiritual hardness blocks the Word of God, however well preached. So there needs to be some 'dynamiting', to make an opening in the stone walls of hearts, that the message may get through. None of us can open minds and hearts that are spiritually blind or

113

closed. Only God can. We should pray before such a service and during it, and, if possible, pray for specific people. Evangelism is the spearhead of the attack on the powers of Satan, so the battle will be fierce.

Similarly we will pray for this 'opening of doors for the Word' when we go out in evangelism on the street or door-to-door. When I served in Holy Trinity, Platt, in Manchester we organized the parish into four quadrants. If you lived in one of the quadrants then that area was your particular spiritual responsibility. If you lived outside the parish, you were designated to one of the quadrants. There were leaders for each quadrant with autonomy of strategy. But all the quadrant teams met regularly to pray for the streets in their area by name, for people living in those streets by name, for shopkeepers by name; the work of contact, visiting and house meetings was undergirded with prayer for 'open doors' in people's hearts.

How much prayer is needed like this for the particularly hard areas for the Gospel – the inner city areas, or those parts of the world where nationalistic religions hold sway over people. You may feel your place of work or the area where you live is hard too, because of materialistic self-satisfaction. We can pray that God will open doors for the Gospel and that we and others may share the Gospel clearly.

3 FOR THE WORD OF THE LORD TO TRIUMPH

2 Thessalonians 3.1: 'Pray for us, that the word of the Lord may speed on and triumph'. This had happened amongst the Thessalonians, so they knew what Paul was talking about – that breakthrough which brings not a trickle but a flood of people turning to the Lord. Of course, this is what we all long to see. Yet often we get depressed as we read of apparent 'success' stories in other churches or in Christian work elsewhere in the world and feel we are getting nowhere. We then lose the expectancy of faith and grow cold in the expectancy of prayer.

Yet what is the measure of 'success' and failure? Take the situation where the work is small numerically in a tough, depressed area of the inner city. To see a handful of people come through to faith in such circumstances is a triumph. We should not get obsessed with numbers. Your church may not be like X or Y, but does that matter? God has called you *there*. He has called you to serve him and to trust him. Pray, and get others to pray, that 'the impossible' may become the possible, that the Word of God may speed on and triumph, that people in the district may begin to recognize that lives are being changed and that the Gospel *is* the only answer to man's need.

Where the speeding-on and triumph is in large numbers, there is a particular thrill about it all and particular opportunities of bringing unbelievers to witness the evidence; but there are considerable responsibilities of care and training too, as has been discovered in the dramatic advance of the Gospel in South America in recent years.

So let us pray like this for the area where we live, for our town, for our country, for our world. We want to see the Word speed on. We want to see it triumph. And we want those outside the faith to see it too, so that they do not relegate Christianity to the garbage can as irrelevant, but see it as powerfully relevant to today's man in today's world – and relevant to *them*.

4 FOR THE SERVANTS OF THE LORD TO BE PROTECTED

2 Thessalonians 3.2-3: And pray 'that we may be delivered from wicked and evil men; for not all have faith'. Paul knew everything about opposition to the Gospel, with plots against his life, mob violence and all sorts of dangers. His request for 'protection prayer' comes out of vivid experience. Since he wrote those words, the roll of Christian martyrs has had hundreds of thousands added to it, right up to our present day. The pioneer missionary is particularly exposed to the danger of attack. We bow in salute to the courage and zeal that has led thousands to go with the Gospel to cannibal tribes, to dense jungle areas where people live in animistic fear, to areas of danger and disease.

We salute too all who have refused to deny Christ in countries taken over by atheistic powers.

Our prayer for protection must recognize that God's glory may be in martyrdom (and Paul saw that himself in his letters to the Philippians, longing that Christ should be honoured whether by his martyrdom or his deliverance). But, as with healing, we pray for protection and entrust the servants of the gospel to the Lord's care. Many are the stories of remarkable deliverance, of people being stirred to pray – even being woken from sleep to do so – at the very moment that a missionary was facing death and how the attacker has stopped and even has 'seen people standing around the missionary'. In 1979 there was the amazing deliverance of Bishop Deqhani-Tafti in Iran, when his attackers fired at him in bed at point blank range, and the shots ringed the pillow but did not hit him. This, he said, was because so many were praying for his protection. Nevertheless, there are many who have been equally prayed for who, in God's purposes, have been enrolled in the list of martyrs. The Bishop's own son was tragically murdered in Iran in May 1980.

We will also pray for our fellow-Christians in spiritually 'dangerous' moments of their life. One such 'moment' is when a young Christian leaves home to go to university or college. Suddenly all restraints are lifted. Around them are fellow-students with utterly non-Christian ideas on life and morality. It is a moment of self-awareness, of having to make one's own decisions, of being able to do almost anything one wants. Young Christians can be destroyed in the first months, or they can mature, making the faith and its practice 'their own' in a new way. The church at home needs to pray specifically and constantly for its young people in those first vital months of college life, or of leaving home for any reason.

5 FOR MORE TO BECOME SERVANTS OF THE LORD

Jesus looked out on the crowds, in Matthew 9.36-38, and said: 'The harvest is plentiful, but the labourers are few; pray therefore the Lord of the harvest to send out labourers into his harvest'. That is a command to obey. The Church of God across the world always needs more who will truly serve. There are many who help when it suits them, or serve as it fits in with their other interests, but not so many who have pledged themselves as servants of Christ, to whom Christ is first in their lives, who fit their own interests around Christ and service for his kingdom. Pray for more Christians to have such commitment.

Then we must pray for the Lord to call men and women out of their 'secular' occupation, to leave their modern-day fishing nets: their computer programming, their executive position in commerce, their teaching or whatever, and to become set apart as ordained ministers, or missionaries, or serving in relief organizations, or in social care and youth organizations. There is a lessening of such commitment in our day. The opposite needs to happen. So pray, as the Lord told us to do, that he will call more (we cannot call ourselves) and that those who hear the call may say willingly, 'Here am I; send me'.

These five areas of prayer for the servants of the Lord by no means exhaust the range of such prayer, but I hope they may be guidelines. Support for one another in serving Christ is an essential part of being in the Body of Christ. Do not let us fail one another in interest, care and practical help; but supremely we must not fail one another in prayer.

With Samuel (1 Samuel 12.23) let us say to fellow-servants: 'Far be it from me that I should sin against the Lord by ceasing to pray for you'.

17 PRAYER FOR LEADERS, UNBELIEVERS AND ENEMIES

1 FOR LEADERS IN THE WORLD

How do we pray for the world? Primarily, it seems from 1 Timothy 2.1-4, by praying for its leaders and for all in authority: 'I urge that supplications, prayers, intercessions, and thanksgivings be made for all men, for kings and all who are in high positions, that we may lead a quiet and peaceable life, godly and respectful in every way. This is good, and it is acceptable in the sight of God our Saviour, who desires all men to be saved and to come to the knowledge of the truth'.

This praying is not confined to *Christian* kings and rulers. It sees the need to pray for all in authority. That includes military dictators and atheistic rulers as well as democratic governments and godly leaders. God's ability to use a heathen leader for his purposes is dramatically demonstrated in his choice of Cyrus, describing him in Isaiah 44.28 as 'my shepherd and he shall fulfil my purposes' and in Isaiah 45.1 as his 'anointed, whose right hand I have grasped'.

Prayer for leaders requires a world vision, a sense of history and an attention to detail. World vision comes by keeping ourselves informed and by deliberately avoiding mere parochialism in our prayer concern. A sense of history will stop us from expecting too much too quickly, as well as being alert to the suddenness with which events can happen on the world scene. We will try to perceive the long-term purposes of God. An attention to detail will avoid our being vague. Information on the countries of the world and their leaders is available, enabling us to pray by name for rulers and to have some understanding of the political structures of a country. Similarly, in praying for people who wield enormous influence in commerce, trade unions or

118

politics, it is good to pray with names. Ask God to lay particular names on your heart for prayer.

What do we pray about? Certainly not for their well-being or success. We pray for leaders because of their effect on countries. Are we then praying for justice, peace and economic stability? This may be part of the prayer, but the 'movement' of 1 Timothy 2.1-3 leads us on to the spreading of the Gospel as the supreme objective of our praying. God desires all to be saved and to come to the knowledge of the truth. Ideally that takes place in a godly and respectful environment, and in an atmosphere of peace. Of course, the Gospel can flourish under persecution, the blood of martyrs being the seed of the Church, but often an atheistic or oppressive regime endeavours to block the spread of the Gospel. We see this with the 'dissuaders' around Christian churches in Russia, the closing of churches and restriction of real Christian liberty in many countries, the obliteration of Christians amongst the millions murdered in Cambodia and the long suppression of Christianity in China's cultural revolution, although a new day has begun to dawn over that nation.

The need to pray for a 'godly and respectful' society is equally with an eye to the spread of the Gospel. Countries involved in revolution, anarchy, deep unrest, corruption, or religious nationalism, are not easy arenas in which to preach Christ, even if such circumstances make some people turn to Christ. Gathering people together can be restricted, pastoral oversight difficult and publishing limited, but particularly there can be a ban on seeking conversions (and so of evangelistic preaching) because turning from the religion so closely linked to the nation is like becoming a traitor.

A 'respectful' society endeavours to respect the views of others without restricting their freedom to disseminate what they believe, unless what they are saying is itself seeking to restrict freedom. The 'respectful' society enables dialogue to take place and for people to listen to others over any issue. In this atmosphere the sensitive evangelist and witness can flourish and the reasonableness of the Gospel can be explained, away from white-hot bigotry or anger.

The 'respectful' society is concerned about human rights *and* responsibilities, about justice, about the poor and about the environment. God is concerned about these matters too, and so the Christian is able to demonstrate his faith and convictions in tackling such issues.

This then encourages us to pray more consistently and widely for those in authority in the world. We are concerned for peace and for a godly and respectful society and so we will pray for leaders involved in the arms race, the build-up of nuclear power and international relationships. The world stands all the time near the brink of holocaust. Some think the world will submit to Marxist domination for the sake of peace, but that would be a long, long way from a 'godly and respectful' peace. There is much pessimism about the future. The Christian must meet it all with prayer. A new surge of prayer for the world's leaders is urgently necessary, for the sake of peace and thus for the sake of the spread of the Gospel of Christ.

2 FOR UNBELIEVERS

There is a passion in Paul's prayers for his own people, his 'kinsmen by race', that challenges us in our prayers for those near and dear to us – in our families, work-place or country – who have not come to faith in Christ. There is nothing cool about this: 'I have great sorrow and anguish in my heart. For I could wish that I myself were accursed and cut off from Christ for the sake of my brethren, my kinsmen by race' (Romans 9.2-3), or about this: 'My heart's desire and prayer to God for them is that they may be saved.' (Romans 10.1)

As Christ looked at the crowd and saw them as 'sheep without a shepherd' and Paul looks at his kinsmen with anguish because they are not saved, so, surely, we look at our relatives and close friends with deep agony of heart if they are outside Christ. It hurts, deeply. Although they may be delightful people – kind, generous and welcoming – yet they have resisted or rejected Christ.

It will be natural for us to pray much for their conversion. This will usually involve considerable perseverance and patience. Our very closeness to them makes witness more delicate, so we turn to prayer. We will concentrate such prayer on a limited number so that we can give time. This will often mean that it is restricted to family and close friends, but where possible we ought to take on our hearts other specific people, perhaps named to us by missionaries or by people involved in some other section of the Church's work and this will require the information that enables our prayer to be meaningful, loving and specific. It is battle prayer, and the battle is for eternal souls. We may often be the major instrument of prayer for them and so it is a responsible and heart-agonizing task.

If we follow Paul in Romans 10 we will learn to discern the blocks to the gospel that exist in a person (e.g. their view of the Church; their shallow rejection of the Bible as 'fairy tales'; 'science has disproved religion') and then make those blocks our target in prayer and, where possible, action. The blocks may align with the two Paul could see in his kinsmen:

(a) They were ignorant of God's way, the Gospel.
(b) They relied on their own ideas and own way.

Prayer for them would take this up:

(a) Praying that their ignorance might be penetrated, that they might actually 'hear' and understand something of the Gospel through a broadcast, a friend's comment, someone at the office, a book, a traveller on the same aeroplane, or by one means or another. It is *not* that they are usually anti-God or anti-Christ but that they are *ignorant* of the Gospel, however knowledgeable about other things.

(b) Praying that their reliance on themselves might be shaken, that a chink may be made in their self-defensive armour and that they may begin to see the uselessness and emptiness of man's way.

We must always be at the ready but never try to force God's pace or do his work. The father did not pursue the prodigal son, but as soon as the son turned, he ran to meet him. If we discern a turning we must run to welcome, but with care. The prodigal *returned* to the father. For our relatives or friends it will all be new, and if they are older they will find it embarrassing to turn to Christ after so long.

Our sensitivity in love, care and fellowship will be vital. Our insensitivity could be fatal. At such a moment we will need to pray for ourselves as much as the new believer!

The encouragement to go on praying for relatives, friends and others outside the kingdom is the encouragement Paul laid hold of (Romans 10.13): 'Everyone who calls upon the name of the Lord will be saved'.

3 FOR ENEMIES

In the hymn 'What a friend we have in Jesus' these lines occur:

> 'Do thy friends despise, forsake thee
> Take it to the Lord in prayer.
> In His arms he'll take and shield thee
> Thou wilt find a solace there'.

It is all rather 'twee' – an expression of 'Christianity for our comfort'. Certainly, retreat and comfort are part of the Christian experience, but so are attack and discomfort! Jesus does not tell us to 'take *it* to the Lord in prayer' but to take *them* to the Lord in prayer. That is attack rather than retreat!

The charter to pray for our enemies comes from our Lord Jesus in Matthew 5.44: 'Love your enemies and pray for those who persecute you'. That really is a revolutionary way of living. When I want revenge or justice and feel like hitting out, I am to love and pray – and pray, not for myself, but for the enemy who is persecuting! That means praying for members of our family or friends who despise our faith and make sly cutting remarks: It means praying for the person at work who is always getting at us for being 'religious' or 'churchy'; for the lecturer or teacher who constantly makes derogatory remarks about 'naive Bible-bashers'; for the active anti-Christian groups in our area; for oppressors in atheistic countries; for persecutors in the prison-camps of a pagan dictatorship.

Why should we pray for them? 'So that you may be sons of your Father in heaven', says Jesus, 'for he makes his sun rise on the evil and the good, and sends rain on the just and the unjust'. Are we similarly able to share our love with enemies as well as friends? To be happy that our enemies have had a good holiday rather than wishing it had been a disaster? None of us finds this easy, but it becomes easier when you pray for them.

Soon after Bishop Festo Kivengere escaped from Uganda in the Idi Amin dictatorship he came to a Three-Hour Service at our church, All-Souls. It was during a message on 'Father, forgive them; for they know not what they do' that 'a great searchlight' shone in his heart. He felt the Lord telling him to forgive Amin. Festo responded, 'Lord, I don't hate this man' but he felt the Lord telling him that he had been growing hard towards Amin and that Amin was not the loser but Festo. It was a shock for Festo. Then, the Lord said: 'You think it's hard to forgive him? Suppose on that day when the soldiers were putting the nails into my hands, one of them had been President Amin with a hammer and nail. Would I have said: "Father, forgive them all except Amin?" 'That was enough,' wrote Festo. 'It was all I needed. I bowed my head and said, 'Please, Father, forgive me, forgive me! Then give me grace to forgive President Amin'. He did. That's why the little book *I love Idi Amin* could be written.

How many enemies or persecutors are on our prayer lists? When did we last seek to love and pray for those who laugh at our faith? When have we needed to pray, and been able to do so: 'Father, lay not this sin to their charge'. Only hearts flooded with the love of God can pray like this. I know how much I fail in such praying. Perhaps you feel like that too. If so, let us pray for ourselves that we may follow the example of our Lord Jesus, of Stephen, of Festo Kivengere, and have grace to forgive, to love and to pray for our enemies and persecutors.

18 PRAYER FOR THE CHURCH

Alongside the many glorious aspects of the Christian Church, there will always be things wrong with it, because it is made up of sinful people, and that includes us! We cannot opt out. We have been baptized by the one Spirit into the one Body. We are involved and cannot be a mere spectator. We all long for the Church (the body of believers across the world) to be more glorifying to God and more effective as God's agent to the world. We will work to forward these aims but we must also pray.

Our Lord Jesus showed us how to pray for the Church, in his great 'high-priestly' prayer of John 17, a prayer of unfathomable depth and multiple richness. There are at least five major themes that we can adopt from it as prayer-targets, in praying for the Church:

1 THE 'SET-APARTNESS' OF THE CHURCH

'Yours they were, and you gave them to me.' (verse 6) 'I am praying for them; I am not praying for the world but for those you have given me, for they are yours'. (verse 9) 'All mine are yours, and yours are mine, and I am glorified in them.' (verse 10) 'They are not of the world, even as I am not of the world.' (verse 14)

The Church often gives the impression of being 'set apart' by ecclesiastical ceremonies, old-fashioned language, out-of-touch ministers and almost total irrelevance to modern living. Such impressions are often unfair, although we have to admit that they can also be accurate. The evidence that the Church is the 'people of God', a group of men and women united in their love for God the Father, saved through the blood of Christ and renewed by the Holy Spirit, glorifies the Lord, as long as the faith is not held on to smugly but shared openly and warmly. The people of God in any area should be known as the carers, as those whose love is active to others in need, to the young

124

and the elderly. The set-apartness of the Church is not negative but positive, as it becomes the hands and feet of Christ in service as well as the Body of Christ in worship.

Pray that the churches we know may be demonstrating this God-powered mark of being his people. It will be seen in their sense of stepping forward. We are the people of *God,* not just a human organization finding itself squeezed by the world into dwindling numbers and ineffective impact. Christ is the head of the Church, leading it and empowering it. We are to look to him for his strategy, his way forward, his leading, so that he can bless us in following him and glorify himself through us, as those who belong to him.

Times away together for the local church or its leaders, when there is real openness to God and a desire to be shown how to alter course, initiate or correct, will keep the church in his will. We have developed these with our staff, our church council and other groups. The results are clearly visible, as the church's navigation is trimmed to what we sense the Lord is saying to us.

We will want to pray that our worship services will have the reality of the people of God met together with him, so that outsiders coming in may sense that we 'mean business' with God and that he is meeting with us and pouring out his blessing. Man-centred, cold, formal and boring services instantly give the opposite impression.

Our prayer will also be that each of us who belongs to God may show that belonging by an increasing grasp of the faith, a readiness to give a reason for the hope that is within us and a relevant application of the faith to daily living. As Jesus says, in verse 3, 'this is eternal life, that they *know* you the only true God, and Jesus Christ whom you have sent.

2 THE SECURITY OF THE PEOPLE OF GOD

'The world has hated them, because they are not of the world.' (verse 14) 'I do not pray that you should take them out of the world, but that you should keep them from the evil one'.

The Church will always be under attack if it is truly 'the people of God' in the world. It is not to retreat into escapist 'holy huddles' (although some will be tempted to do that – in nice, friendly little groups). We are not to be 'out of the world', but in it as salt and light. So Jesus teaches us to pray for security from the Evil One in the battle.

The attacks that come are direct and indirect, with force and with subtlety, from without and from within. The more direct attacks are through political and military force. We must pray for the Church under persecution and in those countries where there seems to have been obliteration of the Church we must pray that the flame of the Church will be kept burning ready to be fanned back into life and witness when a new day dawns. We must pray for the sustaining life of the Spirit for all Christians in prison for their faith, or in countries where the anti-God forces seem rampant, that God's people may be kept secure in Christ.

The evil one also attacks as an 'angel of light' (2 Corinthians 11.14), from within the Church in the form of false apostles and deceitful workmen. Paul was deeply concerned at the way such people attacked the apostolic teaching, diverting people from the true faith with their offers of special spirituality or a less-demanding Christianity. It is painful to us all that people who hold high office in the Christian Church or in university faculties of theology can stab the Church in the back with false teaching, denying even the foundation doctrines of the incarnation and the atonement.

Attacks from outside the Church have come from false cults and heresies since the beginning. In the present day these proliferate with colossal financial backing and an alarming hold over people. The streets of the big cities are their hunting ground, but they also infiltrate the churches. To see young Christians 'captured' by these cults is a sickening experience. To try and rescue those so captured is a heart-agonising task.

Young Christians are prone to attack before they have become firmly established in the faith. The glitter of the world's counter-offers of 'satisfaction', the pressure from the larger crowd of non-believers to conform to the world, the compromising Christian who advises them to grow out of keenness into 'a more adult approach' to Christianity, and the inward desire to be accepted – all this puts them in danger. They are not to retreat from involvement. Prayer is the key to their security and survival.

Let us learn to pray, with Jesus, that the people of God may 'be kept from the evil one'.

3 THE SANCTIFICATION IN THE TRUTH

'Sanctify them in the truth; your word is truth.' (verse 17) 'I have given them your word'. (verse 14) 'I pray also for those who believe in me through their word'. (verse 20)

In the Old Testament the high priest was sanctified externally, by washing, new clothes and anointing with oil. In the New testament, with the 'priesthood of all believers', sanctification is internally, with the truth of God's Word. In John 15.3 Jesus had said to the disciples, 'You are already made clean by the word which I have spoken to you' and went on to say 'If you keep my commandments, you will abide in my love'.

There was deep concern in the early church to 'guard the deposit' of truth, to deliver what had been received, to keep true to the apostles' doctrine. The test of what was included in the New Testament was apostolic authorship or attestation. The New Testament is thus the successor to the apostles and the succession of this apostolic truth is of vital importance to the Church. Where the Church has strayed from the foundation of the Scriptures it has always gone into error and off course. Where it has sought to stand on the Scriptures and to go on studying them with openness it has grown in truth and been more accurately on course.

Our prayer for the Church must therefore be a heart-longing for the spread of the Word of God and the increasing understanding of it by all God's people. We will pray for those involved in translation of the Scriptures, for those seeking to distribute them in forms that make them more readable and for those trying to get more Bibles into countries where the availability of Bibles is limited. It seems incredible to me that many churches, even those who say they 'stand upon the Scriptures and preach the Word', do not have Bibles at every seat, so that stranger or regular can open the Bible together with ease (page numbers being given) and have the passage being read or preached on before their eyes. The response that 'people should bring their own' totally ignores the strangers and their unfamiliarity with the Bible. It is music to a preacher's ear to hear the rustle of the pages of the Bible all over the church because he can then expound and point to the actual text. So I pray for churches to put first things first and to get Bibles for everyone. Better to sit on the floor with Bibles than in pews without them!

We must then pray for the teachers of the Word. It is an awe-inspiring responsibility to preach and teach. That there is often such poor preaching and little exposition in the Church is appalling. I constantly meet lovely Christian people who are sick at heart that they are being spiritually starved in their local church, and they long for preaching that is opening up the Word of God with both depth of perception and relevant application. Pray for such preaching and teaching in the Church everywhere and pray for those who have this responsibility locally. Pray for the leaders of the Church across the world that they may stand on the Word and teach it. Pray too for those who teach the preachers in theological colleges. Pray for a deep submission to the Word and a sitting light to tradition.

All this, however, is ineffectual unless the Word is heard, received and fruitful in our lives. The key is in our desire to grow. I am amazed that so often in a Christian student gathering where I have been asked to expound a passage of Scripture at length, most have brought neither Bibles nor note-books. Can they really want to grow? I doubt it. The hearers and learners who want to be sanctified in the truth will take the Word of God seriously – through preaching, teaching, group studies and in personal discipline. The majority of spiritual ailments can be traced back to

carelessness about the Scriptures. If it was not so important, Christ would not have prayed 'Sanctify them in your
truth'. What is important to him must be important to us.
So let us pray anew for ourselves and our fellow-Christians
that we may be hearers and doers of the Word.

4 THE SENTNESS OF THE PEOPLE OF GOD

'As you sent me into the world, so I have sent them into
the world. And for their sake I consecrate myself ... '
(verses 18,19) 'I pray also for those who believe in me
through their word.' (verse 20)

The disciples were to take over the mission of Jesus, and
his heart was deeply in prayer for them. We inherit the task
and its responsibility. Unless the Church has 'sentness' it
will become merely inward-looking and die. It must have
its set-apartness – its worship, fellowship and teaching –
but this must be balanced by sentness, in involvement,
mission and challenge.

Part of the guideline we can follow comes from the phrase
'As you sent me ... so I have sent them'. Jesus became
incarnate, with us bodily. He was involved amongst us,
sharing our life and its experiences, meeting with agnostics,
atheists, hypocrites and enemies; as well as with enquirers,
believers, and disciples. He mixed, he took time with
people, even one-to-one. He could share poverty or sit at
a rich man's table. He was not confined to any one form
or method of evangelism. He adapted his approach
according to the circumstances. He was strategic in action
and timing. And in all this he was constantly aware of his
'sentness': 'My food is to do the will of him who sent me,
and to accomplish his work'. (John 4.34)

'Sentness' for us is thus not confined to missions or
evangelistic efforts (although it includes those), but widens
out to embrace the whole purpose of our life. We are sent
into the world – in the insurance office, the sports club, the
car-assembly line, the street. All we do is as God's people,
and wherever we go and whatever we do, it is as those sent
by the Lord. There is no room for separation between our
business life and our Christian life; no place for living a

double life. Our membership of the Body of Christ is to pervade our whole life. This is something to pray for as we range our mind across all the members of our local church, and over the Church in the world. Let us thank God for Christians who are unashamed to be known as Christians and pray for those who keep it hidden. Let us pray that Christian lives may influence by their caring, their integrity and their joy, showing the reality of Christian living in the rough and tumble of everyday life.

Sentness also has a specific mission thrust. Jesus became incarnate, but within that incarnation lay the purpose of his teaching ministry and supremely his sacrifice for the sins of the world. He came to offer eternal life to all who would believe on him. The Church has the responsibility of proclaiming, spreading and arguing that message: life instead of death, salvation instead of perishing, made possible through Christ's death and resurrection. It is not an intrusion into people's privacy to evangelise when we see it as a matter of life and death. The gospel is not one option among many but the gateway to eternal life. It may be more comfortable and less demanding to ignore mission. We may argue that it is not the way for today, or that we should respect other faiths or that it is better to witness by life not by lip. Nevertheless, the task of mission has been committed to the Church. We may not all agree on methods, but if we do not agree that mission is part of the Church's responsibility we disobey the lord of the Church. Let us pray for churches to have a deeper sense of this responsibility. Where they are already involved, let us pray that they may learn more about how to reach out for Christ in their particular area, and where they have lost any idea of mission that they may be shaken by the Spirit out of their inward-looking complacency into costly action.

World mission is a further part of 'sentness' prayer. Prayer support for what is already taking place is vital. Whether the mission involves care for sick bodies or provision for starving people, its centre will always be the greatest need of every man, the need of spiritual regeneration. It is often the front-line of the battle, so prayer needs to be informed and constant. Let us pray also for the continuing concern for world mission by God's Church, that people and finance will be more adequate for the colossal task which Jesus himself initiated.

5 THE 'SEEN-TO-BE ONENESS' OF THE PEOPLE OF GOD

'That they may be one, even as we are one.' (verse 11). (1 pray) 'also for those who believe in me through their word, that they may all be one; even as you, Father, are in me, and I in you, that they also may be in us, so that the world may believe you have sent me'. (verses 20 and 21) ... 'that they may become perfectly one.' (verse 23)

Prayer for the unity of the Church was deeply in the heart of Jesus. As head of the Church, how much it must be on his heart today. Unity is to be as it is in the Trinity (vv. 20,21) and so is not a uniformity but, like the Persons of the Trinity, a unity in diversity. One big denomination is therefore not necessary. Agreement across the denominations, agreement in the truth of God's Word and in godly love, that shares freely at the Lord's Table, that co-operates in local concerns, that does not compete on the mission field, *is* possible and must be a deep concern of our hearts in prayer. We will pray for unity in the essentials (for it can never be at the expense of truth) and for an openness that accepts the diversity of non-essentials. We will pray for the ability to see which is which!

This unity is also important in the local church. We are to 'endeavour to keep the unity of the Spirit in the bond of peace'. That requires action as well as prayer. We must work at bringing understanding between older and younger, traditional and modern (e.g. in musical tastes), employer and employee and between those of different ethnic backgrounds. We must work at retaining fellowship, support and understanding between leaders in different sections of the church's life. As we work at it, we must pray. The reason for such unity is its testimony to the power of Christ among us, 'that the world may believe you have sent me'. (v. 21) Similarly the 'New Commandment' that we should love one another given in John 13.34,35 is that 'by

131

this all men will know you are my disciples'. So the aim of unity is not first that we may enjoy blessed fellowship (even though this will be a pleasant by-product) but that the Church's witness may be advanced and not blunted. The Church is meant to be a non-selective group of all sorts of people: old, young; rich, poor; healthy, sick; introvert, extrovert; single, married; intelligent, simple; fulfilled, frustrated; modern, traditional; sports-loving, book-loving; handsome, plain. Put that lot together and the sparks *must* fly: and if they don't fly, but the members of such a group actually love one another, the only possible explanation is supernatural. It is powerful evidence of the transforming effect of belonging to Christ and being changed by his Spirit. That makes our prayer for unity more important and makes it prayer for a 'seen-to-be-oneness'; that the witness of this unity may be *seen* by non-Christians, showing them the reality of Christ as living Lord amongst his people.

Many of us long to see the Church more true to its Lord, more true to his Word, more powerful in its witness, more effective in its caring, more loving in its fellowship. So let us do all *we* can as part of the Church to forward these aims, but let us primarily pray for the Church, locally, nationally and internationally, that it may more and more glorify Jesus Christ, its Lord.

POSTSCRIPT

Now – over to you! This little book, with all its inadequacies, is useless unless it affects the prayer-life of its readers. It has affected mine. I hope it will yours, perhaps by a radical overhaul, or by practical action in purchasing a loose-leaf book and beginning a prayer diary, or by learning to 'breathe' prayer or in taking up some fresh emphasis. There is so much more for us all to learn and know about the amazing privilege of praying to the God of heaven and earth and the effectual power of such praying, through the name of Christ and in the power of the Spirit. All prayer starts and ends with God, so:

'Rejoice in the Lord always. I will say it again: Rejoice! Do not be anxious about anything, but in everything, by prayer and petition, with thanksgiving, present your requests to God. And the peace of God, which transcends all understanding, will guard your hearts and your minds in Christ Jesus'. (Philippians 4.4,6,7; NIV)